Sharing not Staring

21 interactive whiteboard lessons
for the English classroom

Second edition

Trevor Millum and
Chris Warren

Routledge
Taylor & Francis Group

LONDON AND NEW YORK

Second edition published 2014
by Routledge
2 Park Square, Milton Park, Abingdon, Oxon OX14 4RN

and by Routledge
711 Third Avenue, New York, NY 10017

Routledge is an imprint of the Taylor & Francis Group, an informa business

First edition published by the National Association for the Teaching of
English (NATE) 2008

British Library Cataloguing in Publication Data
A catalogue record for this book is available from the British Library

Library of Congress Cataloging in Publication Data
Millum, Trevor.
Sharing not staring : 21 interactive whiteboard lessons for the English
classroom / Trevor Millum, Chris Warren. — Second edition.
pages cm. — (National association for the teaching of english (nate))
1. English language—Study and teaching. 2. Interactive whiteboards.
I. Warren, Chris. II. Title.
LB1576.M527 2014
372.6—dc23
2013042613

ISBN: 978-0-415-71639-0 (hbk)
ISBN: 978-0-415-71640-6 (pbk)
ISBN: 978-1-315-77948-5 (ebk)

Typeset in Sabon
by Swales & Willis Ltd, Exeter, Devon, UK

MIX
Paper from
responsible sources
FSC
www.fsc.org   FSC® C013056

Printed and bound in Great Britain by
TJ International Ltd, Padstow, Cornwall

Contents

Preface

Interactive whiteboards and the teaching of English

The advent of the interactive whiteboard (IWB) has opened up really exciting possibilities for the classroom. It is a technology that quite explicitly mimics the teaching tools of the past, bringing a whole bundle of methods together: the blackboard (or whiteboard); the flipchart; the television; the slide projector; the OHP; and latterly the digital projector. As such, it doesn't cancel out long-cherished teaching styles, but attempts to replicate them and create a fusion. Mid-lesson, if we so choose, we can switch to another approach, literally at the touch of a button. The computer linked to the Internet brings 'point of need' teaching within reach, with vast and varied resources at our fingertips.

Even if the IWB stopped there, it would have made a significant enhancement to the potential slickness and pace of a lesson. However, the word 'Interactive' in the title suggests that there is more to explore than simply serving up old lessons dressed in a bright new fashion. Indeed, if we do stop at the surface level of what's on offer, we run the risk of significantly under-using this new and expensive resource. The worst scenario is that the mesmeric power of image and projector will reinforce poor teaching styles, making the tediously didactic into the super-powered didactic. In addition, the technology can be misused: software created that is reductive, banal and ultimately damaging to real education. It is therefore imperative that we approach the IWB with a fresh and more ambitious set of demands than simply treating it like a souped-up blackboard or a computer writ large.

The approaches advocated in this book attempt to establish and encourage best practice in the following areas:

- A transfer of power from teacher-at-front (the so-called 'Sage on the Stage'), to students. This can involve simple physical participation at one end of the scale or a complete reversal of roles at the other. Here students use the technology to support and empower their own presentations, effectively becoming the teacher for a short while – a hugely powerful technique – while the teacher abdicates the spotlight role to become the 'Guide on the Side'.

- A thorough, subject-focused exploration of the interactive potential of combining display technologies with a computer.
- The encouragement of techniques that intrigue, puzzle, and ultimately draw students into the excitement of learning.
- A preference for approaches that add to the grip or pace of a lesson.
- An emphasis on creativity, enlightenment, stimulus and animation.
- Quite explicit focus on words; though we do include the use of images, this is a book for the everyday working English classroom, and our business is overwhelmingly with the way *words* work.
- A deliberate attempt to make every suggestion a practical possibility for most teachers, and without the need to purchase special software.
- A concentration on techniques that value the question more than the answer and debate more than a wrong/right polarisation. (We feel uncomfortable with voting systems, for example, unless they are used as *opinion-gathering systems* where there is no right answer.)

We have divided the ideas into the following broad categories which mostly cover the points above.

Spotlight and word cover/reveal effects

- Variously deployed, these approaches have the impact of a puzzle; they emphasise the question as opposed to a pat answer.

Text organisation

- The IWB makes sequencing and the exploration of syntax not only possible, but exciting.

PowerPoint

- The ubiquitous tool of the classroom, sometimes overused or misused, has much creative potential as a highly versatile piece of software.

Word

- Every teacher has access to a word processor of some sort, and most have Word. Combined with the IWB, Word can perform the equivalent of conjuring tricks in the classroom. You can animate text, map it, organise it, hide it, scramble it, unscramble it and generally make rabbits appear from empty top hats.

Image, moving image and Flash

- There is no doubting the impact of a well-chosen still image or video clip – and if you're lucky and you know what you're looking for, you can find many such resources free on the Internet.
- Flash programs that have specific applications with words can add to the wonder and magic of English – but beware of the hackneyed 'drag and drop' which often reveals a failure of the designer's imagination or a poor understanding of English. Look for programs that liberate or surprise.

Timers, choosers and other engagement tricks

- Setting a time for a task, or having a timed element in a quiz activity, injects it with tension and excitement. If students don't know who will be 'up next', the anxiety generated again adds a dynamic to the lesson, adding to the perceived fun.

The activities described can be undertaken with any of the popular brands of interactive whiteboard. Given their widespread use, we have at times made specific reference to the Smartboard or Activboard. This does not imply an endorsement of either product or that other boards cannot be used equally well for these activities. Indeed, most of the activities described can be enjoyed with a projector and a computer.

Postscript

When you find yourself in front of a class using an IWB, you'll know that the interface you are using just *has* to be simple. You may have taken time to create quite a complicated resource, but when you're at the sharp end, trying to think about teaching, you won't be able to devote much attention to complex navigation or other IWB logistics. During the writing of this book, we spoke to Dave Martin, the inventor of the interactive whiteboard. He told us that only about 10 per cent of the brain is available for operating the board if you're actively teaching. This has implications for the design and configuration of your resources. Make sure they are really simple, with all the controls at the surface. (For instance, you might take time to re-configure Word so that the full menus are available without annoying short delays and all the toolbars you need are displayed, and, if the software allows it, perhaps that there's a visual display of the stages of the lesson.) Do expect some sudden loss of know-how, those 'where-have-I-put-it?' moments, and try to eliminate them by careful preparation!

Trevor Millum and Chris Warren

Introduction

Interactive whiteboards – a guide to designing effective materials of your own

The context is a familiar one for the classroom: you stand in front of the board and use it to illustrate a learning point to the class. However, if the board is in fact the screen of a computer, two things change: the familiar board-teacher-class context *and* the use of computers as a learning tool.

Problems occur when lessons planned for interactive whiteboards are based on either traditional board use, or a methodology borrowed from conventional uses of ICT, where it was seen as a solitary learning device. Combining these two approaches demands a fresh approach.

First, we need to look at the potential of this technology to enhance the best aspects of both approaches, and then explore where something entirely new is made possible.

If you have an interactive whiteboard in your classroom, there are a number of ways you can organise the space. Each one has implications for the sort of lesson you can teach and for the design of materials to run on the whiteboard. The two principal modes are these:

1 teacher stands at the front of the class and teaches the lesson actively using the whiteboard;
2 teacher stands to one side and encourages members of the class to participate directly, using the whiteboard.

Some lessons will combine elements of both; others will be characterised by just one. But you need to think flexibly about the resource and explore all of its potential.

This introduction discusses the possibilities for each of these contexts, and the design implications that stem from them.

Teacher stands at the front of the class and teaches the lesson actively using the whiteboard

Two things distinguish this scenario from the usual computer-based lesson:

1   the whole class can participate
2   there is a teacher actively operating between the class and the computer screen (in this case, the whiteboard).

Let's look at the implications:

- *Materials for an interactive whiteboard do not have to indicate right or wrong – they should be left open*

The material doesn't have to be right or wrong in the usual, restricted, black-or-white, binary way of computers. Nor does the computer need to indicate whether something is correct – *you* are there to cover that aspect of the lesson and you can withhold the answer or allow alternative lines of thinking to progress, perhaps to allow pupils to develop their own logical approaches.

- *Ideally, there should be deliberate gaps introduced into the lesson – to give room for teacher and pupils*

The materials do not need to be complete – indeed, if the picture is heavily filled in there will not be as many opportunities for class discussion.

- *Add direct questions in the text on screen that can only be answered by the class and the teacher – an open-ended approach*

The questions can act as a simple guide to the issues the teacher wants to raise at various points in the lesson. The words on screen focus the whole class on the question, but the answer must be supplied through discussion and response – it can't be stumbled upon by the random clicking around the screen that sometimes characterises solitary computer use.

- *If you're teaching at the front, don't design whiteboard materials that 'do everything'*

If you do, the lesson will have 'failed' in that you are, by definition, excluded from the process, except as a clicker of buttons and driver of the software. Allow for, and celebrate, teacher expertise.

- *Design lessons where the use of markers can enhance the learning experience*

Again this requires you to insert deliberate gaps. An example might be the use of blank maps so that the class together fill in the information, and the understanding grows from that process. Always leave blank space for notes.

- *Use links and hypertext creatively*

Don't think only in linear ways. It is possible to follow a linear path through a subject for part of the lesson, then reach a crossroads where there are several branches. A computer can easily be programmed to provide those alternative routes, and make each choice a vivid experience. You can explore alternative takes on a single issue in this way, providing the class with dynamic decisions as you proceed.

- *Use loops*

You can use loops as well as hypertext links, so that you design a return to material already covered – another break from the linear lesson.

Teacher stands to one side and encourages members of the class to participate directly, using the whiteboard

There are multiple opportunities for enjoyable class participation with whiteboard technology, but the materials need to be designed consciously for that effect. Ask students up to the front to participate.

- *Pupils present to the class*

This is a typical English oral activity – a talk or speech – but it can be applied to any aspect of the curriculum and any subject. With an interactive whiteboard, new potentials emerge. Individual pupils, or teams, can use ICT presentation tools such as PowerPoint to prepare visually attractive and dynamic presentations for their peers. The strategy provides a strong focus for the team's work. Preparing and performing the presentation itself is a dynamic part of the learning process, reinforcing understanding and developing skills of communication and expression. The scaffolding provided by the technology very often counters reticence and timidity, bolstering confidence and supporting the narrative thread of the discourse with timely bullet points or a pattern of planned prompts. Asking pupils to take on the teaching role, albeit briefly, encourages the maximum engagement with the material; see below.

- *Try semi-competitive activities*

Two groups in class compete through representatives at the front of the class. There are a number of puzzle-type activities that can work for a whole class. A classic example is the computer Snap game that can be adapted for almost any subject.

- *Quizzes*

Some excellent work has been observed using computer quizzes to stimulate a class's engagement with a subject. Seemingly off-putting features of PowerPoint have proved to be surprisingly effective here. Sound effects such as applause, which we would normally avoid, make a communal quiz activity much more lively. Combine quizzes with the use of Timers and you have the basis of an outstanding lesson – but remember that quiz activities sometimes over-emphasise wrong/right and black/white, whereas much of English is about opinion, judgement and the full spectrum of colours, so combine the fun with discussion and debate.

- *Lessons given by the class*

This inversion of the normal role of pupils – to make *them* the teachers – is one of the most powerful approaches available. It switches pupils from passive absorption to active engagement and, as we all know as teachers, lends urgency and focus to the process of learning. Nothing facilitates learning quite so effectively as having to transmit the result to someone else! For instance, in the study of a work of literature, or a topic in science, you may wish to divide the class into teams, each concentrating on a particular aspect. The lesson(s) conclude with each team teaching the whole class. The advantages of this approach are many. The technology makes these mini-lessons much more enjoyable; the whiteboard makes it possible for the whole class to participate (and you may wish to add to the teams' briefs that they must ask questions and engage the class); and each team will have a powerful incentive to 'know its stuff' because failure to come to grips with the material will be embarrassing. You may wish to try the well-established Jigsaw technique here. There are a number of excellent websites devoted to it. Try writing "jigsaw technique" (including the double inverted commas) into a search engine, or simply visit www.jigsaw.org.

- *Whiteboards used to experiment and to focus discussion*

You may wish to ask groups of pupils to the front of the class to experiment, to try things out in front of peers, or to discuss the outcomes and the consequences of certain lines of thought. A lesson doesn't have to be simple transmission of pre-digested, pre-planned ideas – it can be about the creative formation and development of new ideas, or novel rearrangements of existing ones. Whiteboards really empower this approach.

Some general principles

- *Visual lessons.* A huge range of visual images are available on a computer and they are enhanced by introducing movement (this often gives an astonishingly powerful boost to understanding – try scaling important text items by adjusting font size up and down), and through the sheer scale of the image when it's projected on screen. The trick is to design lessons that exploit the power of images: for example, maps, mathematical concepts and diagrams.
- *Pause, Forward and Back in animations.* In the context of an interactive whiteboard, you need to have delicate control over a moving sequence – to stop it mid-movie, and to run backwards or forwards as the needs of the class demand. This will enable discussion to be at your discretion.
- *Cover up and Show.* It is very easy to design activities that work simply on the lift-the-flap principle, where you conceal the answer, and then click to reveal it. Never lead with the answer – always allow yourself to question first – and try to avoid reductive simple wrong/right approaches. For instance, you might set a task to guess a hidden word. When it is revealed, say it is the author's chosen word and ask the class to weigh it up against the words they suggested rather than imply that it is the 'right' answer.
- *Sequences of activities.* The computer lets the lesson-creator assemble a series of linked activities to explore, or reinforce, specific learning objectives. The navigation through these activities can be designed with the whiteboard lesson in mind – especially the ability to backtrack and loop.
- *Simplicity.* Don't be afraid to keep it simple! One of the most effective discussion starters for English is an example of extreme simplicity. One word appears at a time on the screen – the opening sentence of a novel – and each word triggers a fresh debate, and an attempt to predict the next word and to guess the nature of the writing being presented (the so-called 'flight path' of the novel). So simple, but brilliantly effective!
- *Who's doing the work?* As in the example above, design activities where the mental work is done by pupils. Extravagant visual effects and video look lovely, but often disguise poor pedagogical design and very low levels of mental activity in class!

Texts from the Internet

There will be many occasions when you wish to make use of texts you have discovered on a website. If you copy them from a site and then paste them into Word or into the software which accompanies your IWB, you may find that they do not behave as you expected. This is because you have inadvertently copied embedded bits of coding as well as the text. In our experience, the easiest, most foolproof method of dealing with this irritation is to paste the text into Notepad before going any further. (Notepad can be found in Accessories from Start > All Programs.) Once you have pasted the text into Notepad, copy it again and *then* paste it into whichever application you wish to use.

Hide and reveal

The IWB offers a number of methods and applications which all converge on the same effect – a picture is covered up and the teacher or class can control which part is revealed. How this applies to teaching and learning will be discussed later in this section, but the principal methods are these:

- *Use of a 'blind'.* This is an opaque or semi-opaque block of colour that mimics the effect of drawing a curtain over the screen. It is dragged from the bottom, top or sides of the working area and allows the teacher to reveal the picture or text piecemeal, progressively, horizontally or vertically. Blinds are not part of standard PCs – they are packaged with the interactive whiteboard you have purchased.
- *Use of a 'spotlight'.* This feature, again only supplied as part of an IWB package, obscures the screen, revealing only a small circle (the spotlight). Teachers can drag the spotlight around the screen – and make the circle bigger or smaller at will. The effect is quite dramatic, but as with the blind, you cannot have two spotlights on the screen at the same time, so it is used to isolate an item for discussion, allowing the teacher to concentrate attention on something by obscuring all distracting material.
- *Use of PowerPoint.* In PowerPoint you can create variously shaped blocks of colour and drag them over the top of the image you want to obscure. You can set the exact sequence for their removal in advance of the lesson. Simply clicking on the screen will run through this pre-programmed sequence.
- *Use of Word.* Word tables can be pressed into service for this task, and they offer some special advantages if you are prepared to work on the technicalities. A table can be superimposed over an image, and then by choosing Fill or No Fill you can reveal the picture behind – *cell by cell*. This is not pre-programmed as in PowerPoint; the class can choose which cell to reveal next. A pattern of revealed cells can be built up – you're not restricted to one solitary area as in blind or spotlight work. It's a bit like the television programme *Catchphrase*.

Chapter 1

There's more to a picture than meets the eye . . .

We are aware of the important role that visual images play in communication, more so today than at any time previously. While pictures may have been more readily understood by people in pre-literate times when literacy was the preserve of the educated few, the mode of communication would have been predominantly oral. In the 21st century, pictures of all kinds are ubiquitous and yet education in visual literacy is in its infancy.

The digital projector can assist in this, giving us the opportunity to display images quickly and cheaply, but the IWB allows us to go much further – that is, not just to look but to explore and analyse.

Interactive whiteboard technology enables you and your students to:

- explore a picture with the whole class, enlarging or homing in on details as required
- hide an image and explore it, revealing a small section at a time
- enlarge, reduce and annotate images
- prepare pictures with ready-labelled features, such as questions and comments to be used later
- save the results of class discussions for a subsequent lesson or for students to take and use themselves.

LESSON IDEAS

1. Using an image to explore a literary text

Overview

The literary text in this case is Tennyson's *Lady of Shalott* and the image on p. 2 shows how Holman Hunt interpreted it in his painting.

'The Lady of Shalott' by Holman Hunt (Wikimedia Commons)

Explore the painting first using the spotlight tool to uncover small details without revealing the overall picture. This process should raise interesting questions and issues about the content of the picture. The spotlight tool can be set with varying degrees of transparency. A setting of about 10 per cent transparency should allow you to navigate to where you wish to be with some accuracy. Unless you know the painting really well, it's useful to have a print-out to refer to while moving the spotlight from place to place.

When the whole painting is revealed, the wider context can be discussed, including the interpretation which the painter has chosen. Following this, the poem itself can be explored. Alternatively, students can come to the painting having read the poem and be invited to comment on the relationship between poem and picture.

The lesson

Using the spotlight tool, begin by showing students a copy of the image with all except a small detail hidden. Adjust the size of the spotlight to show just enough to stimulate the interest of the class. (A student could be invited up to the screen to describe what can be seen.)

At this stage, keep control of the spotlight – and ask questions rather than suggesting answers. Begin at the edges of the painting and only move to the central character when you feel the context has been explored in sufficient detail.

Bearing the poem in mind, ensure that aspects such as the knight in the mirror and the loom receive attention. Enlarge the size of the spotlight when appropriate – for example, when you begin to look at the Lady of Shalott herself.

Aspects such as historical period, the location and who the characters are could be explored. Holman Hunt and his fellow Pre-Raphaelite painters paid great attention to details, so it is appropriate to ask about the significance of any aspect that catches the attention. When you feel you've spent enough time on details, expand the spotlight beam and discuss the students' reactions as they see more of the whole picture.

Finally, close the spotlight tool to reveal the whole picture. This is probably the time to record some of the comments by annotating the image using the whiteboard pens. Students can help with this. Make sure that the comment is linked to an appropriate part of the image. If you haven't already done so, introduce the poem or extract on a separate page. Students can then place words or phrases from the text beside appropriate parts of the image. In the illustration you will see quotations from the poem together with comments. These can be colour-coded, and you can use further colour-coding to indicate other aspects.

Students could prepare a reading of the poem while a member of their group uses the spotlight to focus attention on particular parts of the image. If computers are available, students could follow this up by annotating their own copies of the painting, using extracts from the text and their own words. They could either use the interactive whiteboard software (which makes it easy to store results in a plenary session), presentation software (such as PowerPoint) or a word processor. If computers are not available, students could work on printed copies of the image and the poem.

You could print out a copy of the interactive whiteboard page complete with the annotations made during the lesson if you wanted to provide prompts.

Even her
hair seems
out of her
control

'He flashed into the crystal mirror,
"Tirra lirra," by the river
Sang Sir Lancelot.'

Men
determine
her fate

She has a
lovely face

She is kept
prisoner by
the loom and
the threads
entangle her

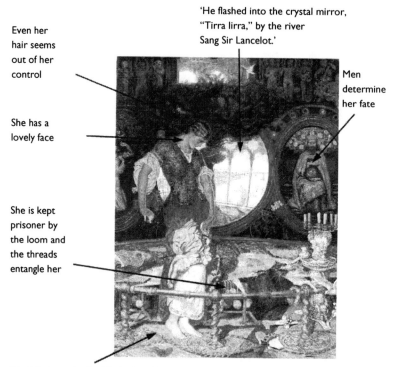

'She left the web, she left the loom'

Tips

- If you don't want the students to see the whole image first, ensure that you activate it on an earlier page then use the page down key to move to the image. Practise this before the lesson so that the spotlight is in a suitable place on the image.
- Always keep a separate copy of the image, and of your interactive whiteboard lesson resource, so that you can use it again later without any changes and annotations made in the lesson. This will also allow you to call up a clean copy of the image for students to work on.

Optional follow-up

Tennyson's poem inspired a number of other paintings and illustrations, including several by Waterhouse. You could invite students to compare them to the Holman Hunt picture shown on p. 2. They could also find out about Tennyson's reactions to Hunt's original representation of this scene, which was for an engraving to accompany an edition of the poem.

2. Visual metaphor

Here is a lesson idea which uses advertising imagery and also serves as a powerful introduction to (or revision of) the way in which metaphor works. This technique can be used with any visual images. Browse through magazines until you find an advertisement where the advertiser is clearly using a visual metaphor. Weekend supplements and women's magazines are rich in examples.

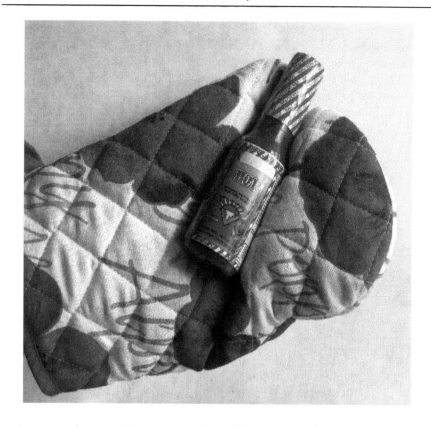

Scan or photograph some samples. Using the technique described on p. 3, shine the spotlight on items such as the rose and ask for the associations (or connotations, if you wish to introduce the term) of roses. Then spotlight the paper towel and ask what possible connection there might be. Students could jot their ideas down before any discussion. Then reveal the complete advertisement which makes the metaphor explicit. Consider several further examples and finish off with the oven glove holding the chilli-hot ketchup. What could be clearer? The sauce is hot! No words necessary. Follow this with some examples of written metaphor or simile to underline the point – and why not ask students to bring in examples of visual metaphor? They make stunning displays.

Resources

Google and Yahoo! have good image search facilities – be as specific as you can with the search terms. Remember when searching for images on the Internet that these are often quite small and enlarging them produces poor-quality display. Using the Advanced Search option (click on the top right icon), you can narrow your search to images above 1024 × 768 pixels or even higher. You can also use your own books and photographs and scan suitable pictures.

Texts can be found on the Internet and copied to use with the interactive whiteboard software, and you can also simply drag selected text from a web page or word processor straight onto the interactive whiteboard page.

Here are a few sites worth visiting for images associated with literary texts:

- There's a useful page on Tennyson's *The Lady of Shalott* on Ed Friedlander's site, including the complete text and a number of paintings: www.pathguy. com/shalott.htm Clicking on a picture loads a high-quality version better suited to use on screen.
- Millais' *Ophelia* is another Pre-Raphaelite painting that repays exploration. *Tate Online* has a good education resource, complete with an extract from *Hamlet* and interesting information about the composition of the picture: www.Tate.org.uk/Ophelia.
- *The William Blake Archive* – www.blakearchive.org – is an excellent source for high-quality images of Blake's engravings.
- You can also take pot luck and search using terms such 'literary paintings' or 'Shakespeare paintings'. Some of the images you, or your students, discover will inspire discussion and could lead to some interesting creative writing.

Chapter 2

Grid reference

Revealing an image a bit at a time can really engage a class. There are a number of methods of doing this, including using Word tables and Word shapes. The premise of this activity is simple. A picture is covered up and the teacher or class gradually reveal it, bit by bit. This can prompt great discussions, and focus attention on specific parts of visual texts. The examples used here are relatively simple. Once you're familiar with the technique you can try making things more sophisticated.

Here is an effective and efficient way of gradually revealing an image in a more controlled way than that offered by the spotlight. It uses the facilities made available in Word when you create a table.

Firstly, choose the image that you wish to discuss: for example, a photograph from a newspaper. Scan or photograph it and store it in a location you will be able to find easily later. You may also wish to change it to a more convenient size.

In Word, create a table, say five columns by four rows, and set the row height so that you have cells roughly the shape that you can see in the example on p. 10. Aim to create a table roughly the same size as your picture.

Select the whole table and then click the small arrow next to the 'Shading' icon (the paint-pot filler). Select a colour. The table will be shaded that colour.

Click the 'Insert' tab, and choose 'Picture'. Browse to find the image you saved previously. Don't worry where the picture is pasted for the moment. It's the next bit which is important.

Right-click on the picture and click on 'Wrap text', then select 'Behind text'. Now slide the picture behind the table. It is easier to use arrow keys to adjust its position.

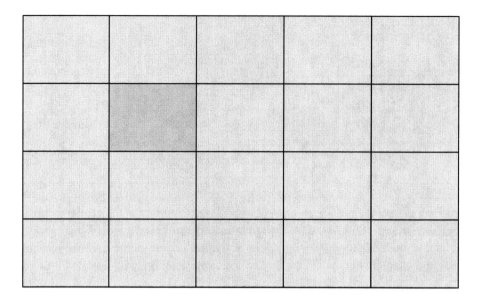

You can make the table fit as closely as possible over the picture either by hovering over the bottom right corner and dragging it to the desired size or alternatively adding more rows. Do this by clicking in the bottom right cell and then pressing the Tab key as many times as necessary.

You are now ready to use your mystery image. Select 'No colour' from the 'Shading' (tipping-paint-pot) icon. Now click on a cell and then on the 'Shading' icon. A segment of the mystery picture appears.

You can, of course, reverse the process and hide cells after they have been seen.

LESSON IDEAS

1. Captions and cropping

Choose a photograph, the 'meaning' of which can be substantially altered according to the caption or headline which is associated with it. Display three or four possible captions and, having revealed a small part of the picture, ask the class to write down which caption they think accompanies the photograph, and why.

Reveal a few more cells and allow students to add to their notes, changing their selection if they wish but without deleting their original ideas. For example:

- Revolutionary heroine mocked by protesting workers
- Veterans admire civil war heroine
- Memorial to Vietnam nurses ready for next week's anniversary
- Lone tourist visits neglected monument

When the picture has been revealed, discuss the importance of captions or headlines to 'anchor' the meaning of a visual image. Move on to other selected images and, subsequently, encourage students to bring in images of their own – perhaps with the captions removed for the class (and you) to discuss.

Another approach focuses on the significant way in which cropping can change the meaning of a picture. A similar approach to the one above can be taken but with different sections deliberately hidden.

For example:

'I cried!' says Michelle, 'but it was a lovely farewell party.'

Good times at farewell bash *or* Guests can't wait to leave as speeches drag on? The two key teaching points here are:

1   how visual images can be manipulated to suit the presenter's point of view without even a hint of Photoshop; and
2   how language can be used to alter what is communicated by a visual image.

Again, if students can find examples from newspapers, magazines or the Internet, the learning will be embedded more thoroughly.

2. Quiz

You can use this controlled revealing of an image to make a test or quiz more engaging. This is a technique used on some television quiz shows whereby a

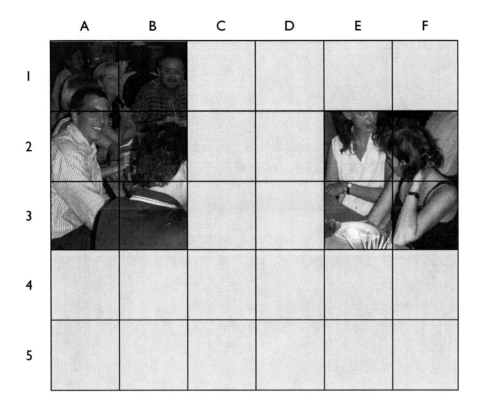

correct answer earns the contestant a piece of the puzzle – that is, one cell of the picture revealed. The team that guesses the nature of the hidden image or the identity of the person is the winner. Having a grid means that students can easily choose the cell they want, for example C3. You might use images associated with a text being studied, and part of a correct answer to the whole picture challenge would be to explain the connection between the image and the text; or, to make it more difficult, having worked out the image, which is then fully revealed, hazarding which text it is connected to.

Tips

- Make sure you prepare this carefully. It's always useful to try something like this on someone before you launch into it with your class. You don't need a whiteboard for that: a laptop will do.
- Always have more images prepared than you think you will need.

Chapter 3

Investigating symbols

Helping students to develop and understanding of the way symbols are used is
a key element in their visual literacy. It will also be useful in their understanding of symbols in both literary and non-fiction texts and can be used in con-
junction with the ideas about teaching metaphor in Chapter 1.

LESSON IDEAS

1. Symbol starters

On p. 16 there is a table with a small collection of symbols as a starting point.
You could photograph or scan it and then project it onto the whiteboard. Use
the annotation function to fill in the blank columns.

These are well-known symbols but will repay some analysis. They are all
what are known as 'conventional' symbols; in other words, there is a convention, often internationally agreed, about what they mean. A flag is an obvious
example of an agreed symbol – without an international convention the green,
white and red of the Italian flag could mean anything.

Some symbols have a visual connection with what they symbolise; others do
not. For example, you could work out that the red line through a cigarette had
something to do with smoking but you would need to know the convention
that a red circle with a red diagonal line indicated: NO/don't do it! You *might*
work out that the three bent arrows had something to do with recycling, but
unless you had been told, you could hardly be expected to know that a white
P on a blue background indicated a parking area. What about the female/male
and the dove?

Symbols used in visual communication need to be understood by the
viewer or they are pointless. There is, though, a continuum from the starkly
obvious (no smoking) through to the deliberately ambiguous. For example, a
sunset could indicate the end of something, a happy situation . . . or perhaps
it is a sunrise? Does a picture of lightning indicate danger, fear or great (natural) power? The same considerations apply when symbols are used in writing.

Symbol	What it is	What it stands for	Where/how it might be used

Symbol	What it is	What it stands for	Where/how it might be used

Here is another series of symbols to discuss and analyse. When you have done so, ask students to start collecting their own examples. These can be used in a class display or scanned/photographed and added to a table in Word for annotation using the whiteboard.

2. Symbols in literature

Some novelists are great users of symbols, but rather than ask students to comb the works of D. H. Lawrence for examples of the moon and its meaning, why not turn to poetry? William Blake's poems are rich in symbols, none more so than 'The Sick Rose'. Here is an example of the way you might use a tabular approach to explore Blake's poem. Students are asked to research pictures for each line and to add a commentary. The whiteboard makes an ideal way to model the process and to display some completed tables. Each row should provoke discussion. For example, should the rose displayed be diseased, or is it, at that point, outwardly whole but sick deep inside?

O Rose thou art sick.		The rose is usually a symbol of beauty. It is also used to signify love — people send roses more than any other flower when they want to convey affection or ask forgiveness.
The invisible worm,		
That flies in the night		
In the howling storm:		
Has found out thy bed		
Of crimson joy:		
And his dark secret love		

Other poems to consider:

- Emily Brontë: 'Spellbound'
- William Blake: 'The Tyger' (and many others)
- Margaret Atwood: 'The Moment'
- Shakespeare: 'Sonnet 116'
- Mimi Khalvati: 'Ghazal'

Film

If you have access to some film clips, it would be interesting to see how film directors handle symbols. Students may not realise how much knowledge they have in 'reading film', and though they may not know the terminology they will probably be able to discuss some of the symbolism in a fairly sophisticated way.

Tips

- Always have plenty of examples to hand. Make a habit of bringing useful magazines or pages from magazines to your classroom and storing them somewhere handy. Use a post-it note to indicate where to find a given image in a magazine and/or the picture's significance.
- If you can access a visualiser, this little piece of equipment is a great way to quickly show everyone an image, which could be from an object such as a drinks can as well as from a page.

Chapter 4

Hidden words

Hiding words encourages discussion, prediction and, most importantly, thought regarding any chosen text. This activity is a variation on the classic 'missing word' task but the use of an IWB enhances the exercise and has practical advantages for learning, not least the fact that it enables the whole class to collaborate on one text at the same time, sharing ideas and developing understanding.

LESSON IDEAS

1. 'Sonnet 130'

This lesson focuses on the rhyme scheme of Shakespeare's 'Sonnet 130'. It works best if students do not already know the poem, since the lesson encourages them to use their knowledge of rhyme schemes and powers of deduction. However, it is also an effective revision activity.

The sonnet is shown to the class with the rhyme words at the end of each line concealed beneath coloured shapes (see p. 22).

Ask your class to predict what lies underneath each shape and justify their response, then slide away the shape to see whether they are correct or not. (Students could also suggest a variety of words that they think might be hidden beneath each shape and test them out.)

Create clones of each shape so that you can add new words and experiment with the students' suggestions. You can then move each alternative word into place in the text and judge whether it sounds and 'feels' right, before comparing your class's choice with the original author's choice.

Ask the students whether each word is 'at home' in the poem: does it suit the tone of the sonnet, as well as the sense, rhythm and rhyme scheme? You may wish to use a rhyme-finder website to provide you with words to test out.

Draw attention to the rhyme words in some way (e.g. by highlighting them or making the font a different colour) so that they are easily distinguished when the text has been fully revealed at the end of the activity.

It is the contribution that the rhymes make to the overall effect which should be stressed – not merely rhyme for rhyme's sake.

Tips

- Double-space the lines in order to avoid the page looking over-crowded.
- Lock the text to the page so that it won't be moved or accidentally deleted.
- Depending on the number of 'clues' you wish to provide for your class, change the size of the boxes to fit the length of the hidden words, or make them all the same size for an increased level of challenge.

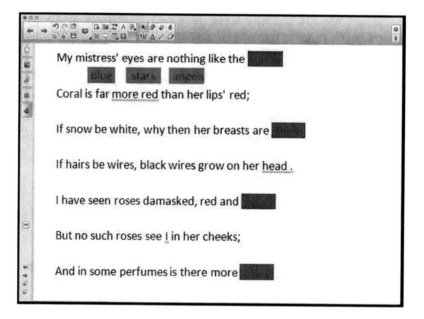

- If computers are available to students, they will be able to work independently on any other sonnet and investigate whether the rhyme pattern they have discovered is common to all sonnets and, if not, what are the most common variants.
- If computers are not available, students could be given paper copies of a variety of sonnets and report back on similarities and differences.

2. Vocabulary building

Hiding words behind coloured blocks can be used for many purposes. It could be used for simple matching activities, as in the memory game of Pelmanism.

In the example, you are trying to encourage students to find alternatives to simple colour words and you have chosen blue, indigo, azure; red, crimson, scarlet, rosy; and green, emerald, jade. A previous student has correctly matched blue and indigo, but the current student has revealed green and crimson and has started to slide the covering blocks back over them.

As with any activity of this sort, it is when the students begin to create their own challenges that deeper learning starts to take place. In groups, ask students to come up with a list of commonly used adjectives and then find two or three alternatives for each.

If they have access to computers, they can create their own hidden word activities using the whiteboard software or PowerPoint.

If they do not have access to computers, they hand their ideas to you and you will have to do the preparation – again! (Unless a couple of students would like to help out over break . . .)

Emphasise that a longer or more complicated word is *not* always the best choice. Sometimes a simple word is exactly what is needed. However, the wider their reservoir of words, the more choice they have when it comes to their own writing.

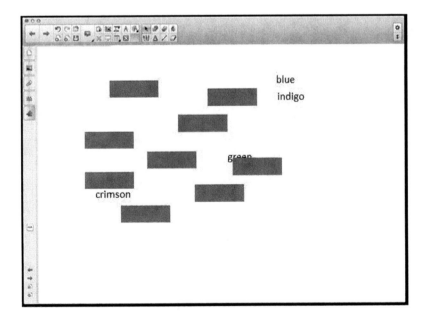

3. Dramatis personae

In this activity, students see an extract from a play with the characters hidden, as in this example from Shakespeare's *Macbeth*:

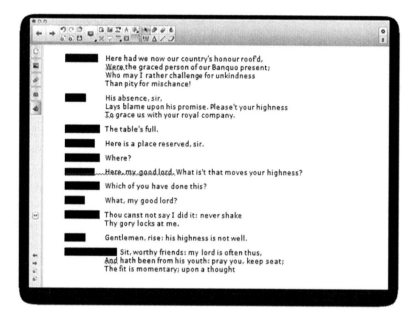

    Having some familiarity with this scene, and working in groups or pairs, students should be able to predict which character is speaking throughout the extract. Having made their predictions, perhaps using a printed version of the scene with the character names blanked out in white to record their decisions, the blocks can be moved to one side. As in the previous activity, a variation would be to have the names on 'tiles' on the right-hand side of the whiteboard to be moved into place. This makes a good revision exercise too.

    Further ideas in the same vein but using a different technique can be found in the following chapter on word walls.

IWB Help

Smartboard

To cover each of your chosen words with a coloured shape, click on Shapes and select one. To colour it, click on the 'Fill' menu and choose a colour. Simply click and drag your cursor over the word or words to be hidden. To create copies (clones) of a particular shape, simply click on the shape so that a blue dotted border appears. Click on the down arrow and then on 'Clone'. Double-click on each shape to type in the alternatives offered by the class – or ones you wish to offer if you are setting up a multiple-choice activity.

Promethean

To cover each of your chosen words with a coloured shape, click on 'Design Mode', select the rectangle and draw a box to suit the size of the word or words you wish to hide. Fill it with a colour and then drag it to where you want it. Keyboard shortcuts Ctrl+C (cut) and Ctrl+V (paste) will create clones. Shapes can be stretched afterwards, if necessary.

Chapter 5

Hidden texts

If hiding words is stimulating, hiding whole texts can be even more so. The technique on which we focus in this section converts any given text into a 'word wall' which is not, in this case, merely a wall with words on, but a wall of bricks behind which the words are concealed. The activities afforded by this technique encourage thinking and discussion about language, structure and text types. Again, the use of the IWB allows the whole class to join in with an investigation and can turn a very ordinary study of a text into an engaging puzzle.

Before going any further, you need to learn how to create a word wall. It will look something like this but yours will be brick red – much more appealing.

If you look closely, you will see a resemblance between the wall and the first paragraph. The first brick is very small: that's because it's hiding the word 'If' – and so on. If this were a live Word document being projected onto your whiteboard, you would be able to select any of the bricks and reveal the hidden word. If you wished, you could then hide it again. This makes the technique a really powerful tool with which to analyse a text or to revise it.

To make a word wall, open Word and find a copy of the text you wish to convert into a word wall.

First double-space the text (select the text, hold down Ctrl and press 2). Select the text and change the font colour to red. Make sure it is the standard red and not a slightly different shade. Then, with text still selected, use the highlighter tool,  also set to red to highlight the whole passage. Your text will now look something like this:

Now comes the tricky part. Go to 'Find and Replace' and open the dialogue box. Click on 'More' and the box will double in size. (Clicking on 'Less' will reduce it again.)

Type a single space where it says 'Find what:' and then place your cursor in the 'Replace with:' area. Now click on the 'Format' button at the bottom left:

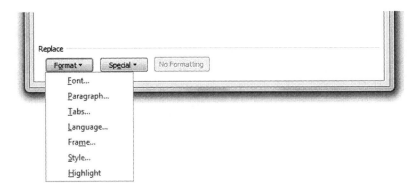

Click on 'Highlight', and the word 'Highlight' should appear underneath the 'Replace with:' area. Now do the same thing again and the words 'Not highlight' should appear. Click on 'Replace All'. What this does is to convert all the long blocks into word-length bricks. You have your word wall. Save it to use when you wish.

When you are ready to use a word wall, select the highlighter tool and then double-click on a brick:

To hide the word, double-click again. You can replicate this on the IWB, of course, and you will find that many students will enjoy coming and interacting directly with the text in this way.

Tips

- Make sure your text is a clean copy – in other words, not downloaded directly from the Internet because such texts often bring with them unwanted bits of code (from frames, cells, etc.) which can prevent things working as you expect. Either use the 'Paste' option 'Keep text only' or past the text into Notepad first and then copy it from there into Word.
- If you can't see any mortar between the rows of bricks, select the whole wall and increase the line spacing. A quick way to do this is Ctrl and 5 (which sets the spacing at 1.5 and seems, visually, about right).

LESSON IDEAS

1. Word wall challenge

Imagine that you are approaching examination time and you need to revise some poetry with your students. Not only that, you want to do it in a way that will engage them and challenge them. A word wall will enable you to carry out a range of activities which seem more like games or puzzles than work.

Divide the class into teams and display the poem on the whiteboard. You might tell them which poem it is or you might get them to guess, based on the shape of the text. Team A gets to choose a brick and guess the word. If they are correct, they gain a point. Team B then has a go, and so on. There will be a series of correct guesses at some stages as a familiar line is recalled, but there will also be halts and pauses where the class gets stuck.

You can vary the rules to suit your students. You may wish to have some words already showing in order to give a few clues. You might also allow a team which has made a correct guess to have another go. This could, conceivably, lead to one team reciting the whole poem, of course! If you think this is a potential problem, limit the 'bonuses' to five. You might like to join in yourself and see how good your recall is.

To make this more than an exercise in remembering, encourage students to look for clues in the meaning of lines to help them estimate the nature of the next word in a line, for example. Also, add casual questions as you go along – 'And what does he mean by that, do you think?' or 'Before we go on, what's the bending sickle?' – which might merit a bonus point.

2. Looking at text types

A similar technique can be used to investigate text types. Rather than present-
ing a text and asking 'What kind of text is this?' and then pointing out the features special to that type, present a text or text extract and investigate it word
by word. Students can choose which brick to remove and make suggestions as
to the kind of text it might be, gathering evidence as more words are revealed.

You may wish to ban certain words from being revealed because they give the game away too quickly, as in this example.

This extract comes from the directions and other information on the packet of a hot chocolate drink. The words which are in black give the name of the product and are, for the purpose of the activity, currently 'out of bounds'. You may wish to place other give-away words under the same restrictions. It is the puzzling over clues and making deductions from the linguistic evidence that leads to learning, rather than being given a unappetising, pre-digested list of five or six points about persuasive or instructional writing!

Chapter 6

Mystery texts

As we have already pointed out, natural curiosity is a good tool to use to engage students with a text. Students may be more interested by a text which is hidden than one which they can see. Exploring texts that disappear or are hidden is like working on an archaeological dig! We can exploit this quirk of human nature to involve students of all ages and abilities in the investigation of texts. ICT gives us a way of making texts instantly invisible and enables us to reveal the text bit by bit. This allows us to focus on aspects of the text such as:

- the period in which it was written
- the type of text it seems to be
- sentence structure
- vocabulary
- a combination of these.

LESSON IDEAS

1. Word dig

The mystery text shown on p. 34 comes from Charles Dickens's *Oliver Twist*. In this lesson we gradually reveal different parts of the text to investigate how Dickens uses language to depict action and drama. Good questioning is crucial. Students should be encouraged to make hypotheses about the text. Reveal the full text when you think the time is right.

Locate the text you wish to use and display it on the IWB using Word.

Select all the text (Ctrl+A) and then set the font colour to white. This will have the effect of making your text disappear. You could use different colours as long as you also change the background colour to the same colour. (Background colours are set in the 'Page Layout' tab by selecting 'Page Colour'.)

If you *select* all the text, its overall shape will be revealed. Students will see that it consists of five paragraphs, one of which is very short. This technique can be used with a variety of texts and a number of deductions can be made even before

any words are seen. To make the effect of the paragraphs clear, you may have to insert extra paragraph returns to increase the spacing between them.

You can return the text to its white-on-white state by clicking anywhere. Now it's up to you which words you decide to reveal – or whether you leave it to chance. There will be some element of chance anyway unless you have an uncannily accurate eye!

A double-click will select one word. Change the font colour back to black – or any other colour as long as it is clear – and the word will now be visible to the class.

    struck   tumbled   The noose

      his   speeds

                   convulsion

Better still, select the black highlighter (in the 'Home' tab) and double-click. Words will then appear like this:

After several words have been revealed, some predictions or deductions can be made. Ask open-ended questions. What kind of text do students think this might be? What is happening?

Continue to reveal words as long as it is fruitful. Reveal the whole text by selecting all of it and either using the black highlighter, or changing the font colour back to black. If you take the latter option, the previously revealed words will now be the invisible ones, as shown below. This may suggest further activities – even if only trying to recall what the missing words were.

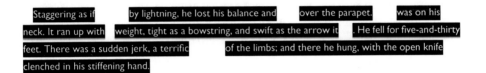

You can either type in your selected text, or scan the text and use character recognition software (usually included with your scanner) to turn the scan into a text document. Many texts can be found on the Internet and copied, but see the Tips box on downloading texts from the Internet in Chapter 5. Once saved, and with the font changed to white, your text is ready to use.

Tips

- Print a copy of the text for your reference so you have some idea where certain words are to be found.
- Having revealed a word using the black highlighter, you can hide it again by clicking once more.
- You can use other highlighter colours. Perhaps you would use one colour to pick out verbs, another for nouns. Or have a blue team and a red team to choose words alternately. Who has the more interesting words? Why?
- Look out for interesting texts in unusual places. Some of the most surprising texts appear in advertising material, on packets in supermarkets, in instruction sheets for electronic equipment and in letters from banks.

---

2. Variations and extensions

Before moving on to reveal more of the passage, or perhaps all of it, students might be asked to use the words revealed so far to create a piece of writing which has to use those words (in the same order, if you wish) plus any others of their choice.

If **students have access to their own computers,** they could afterwards use highlights or other emphases to bring out features of the text they have noted, and add others they think are of interest. For more information on this, see the unit on text-mapping in Chapter 8. As a concluding activity, the class can contribute their suggestions and build up a bank of ideas about the extract – together with any general points about language. **If students do not have access to computers,** they can carry out a similar activity using pens.

Shape recognition

It is quite easy to spot a poem from its outline alone. More than that, it is possible to predict a sonnet or a limerick, just from its shape. What else could be spotted in this way – a play script, a haiku, a recipe?

Your IWB

These techniques work well using any word processing software. However, if you have copied your text onto a Smart Notebook or a Promethean flipchart you can use that tool to carry out these activities in much the same way.

Chapter 7

Tabulate!

Using tables to create interactive resources

Tables are a simple way of organising data. We tend to think of them as things that mathematicians, statisticians and other -icians use, including technicians. Nothing wrong with that – but teachers of English can make good use of them too.

We might use tables to:

- organise – from informal groupings to defined categories
- act as word banks – to hold text to be used in an activity
- compare and contrast – to enable text to be positioned appropriately
- sequence or match.

Lesson overview

You may wish to look at a text in some detail and to analyse the language used. Using tables to enable simple classification adds a slightly different dimension to this kind of activity. The text might be presented in its original form or perhaps be one which you have collapsed into alphabetical order. Either way, you can use tables to help students classify words and phrases:

> He set his foot against the stack of chimneys, fastened one end of the rope firmly round it, and with the other made a strong running noose by the aid of his hands and teeth. With the cord round his back, he could let himself down to within a less distance of the ground than his own height, and had his knife ready in his hand to cut the cord and drop.
>
> At the instant that he brought the loop over his head before slipping it beneath his armpits, looking behind him on the roof he threw up his arms, and yelled, 'The eyes again!' Staggering as if struck by lightning, he lost his balance and tumbled over the parapet.
>
> *(Continued)*

(Continued)

The noose was at his neck; it ran up with his weight; tight as a bowstring, and swift as the arrow it speeds. He fell five-and-thirty feet, and hung with his open knife clenched in his stiffening hand!

The dog which had lain concealed till now, ran backwards and forwards on the parapet with a dismal howl, and, collecting himself for a spring, jumped for the dead man's shoulders. Missing his aim, he fell into the ditch, turning over as he went, and striking against a stone, dashed out his brains.

(from *Oliver Twist*)

Verb phrases	Nouns	Adjectives	Adverbs	
set his foot	brains			
let himself down	stone			
slipping	ditch			
looking behind	shoulders			
threw up his arms	howl			
lost his balance and tumbled	parapet			
	hand			
	knife			

The categories used can be your choice – or theirs. Instead of verbs and nouns, they might decide on words connected with violence, words that are positive or negative, and so on. This way of looking at a text is often more revealing – partly because you don't know what will be discovered. If you look at the passage above, you might discover that a heading for adjectives and adverbs produces, interestingly, rather meagre results. ('Only use an adverb when you cannot find an adequate verb . . .')

If students have access to computers, they can carry out this activity and others like it on their own machines, individually or in pairs.

If students do not have access to computers, provide a print-out for them to work on prior to a plenary session gathering ideas from the whole class and seeing what kind of agreement there is as to the categories.

Further examples

Here's a tried and trusted format for an analysis table which uses a collapsed text that has been filtered for duplicates and grammatical words. (Note that in this example students should invent their own categories. If you do not dictate what those should be, the list will emerge organically with the task. Part of the thinking process involves spotting and naming patterns, without having those patterns imposed by the teacher.) To move a word, simply double-click it and drag it into a box.

bamboo bitter blossom bombs bone bones buds buffalo burned ceremonies charred children clouds delight distinguish dream echo epic fathers flight gardens gathered hearts hold illumined inclined ivory jade joy killed lanterns laughter life light mirrors moonlight more most moths mouth old once opening ornament paddies peaceful peasants people pleasant poem quiet reflected remember reported resembled reverence rice scream silent silver singing sir smashed song sons speech stepped stone tales terraces time told turned water ways were what when whether which who

Create as many categories as you need to sort these words into groups.
You can label the group as you wish, e.g. 'Happy words',
You can put a word into more than one category if you wish.

Above or beneath a text you wish to look at in some detail, create enough cells to accommodate the different categories you might need (though you can always add more if you need them).

In a simple gap-filling exercise, the words to fill the gaps can be placed in a table below the main passage. (Remember to get students to create these themselves too.)

Alongside a text such as a poem or play, create columns that will accommodate 'marginalia', which might be notes on the text or perhaps viewpoints or thoughts:

Banquo's thoughts	The text	Macbeth's thoughts

Lines from a poem, or lines of Shakespeare, will automatically create tables if you select the lines and click on the Table icon. It's then relatively simple to add columns to the right and left.

An advanced version of this idea involves splitting the lines. Here's the first part of a poem where the second part of each line has been moved and needs to be matched correctly:

I met a traveller	stamped on these lifeless things,
Who said:	boundless and bare
Stand in the desert.	and the heart that fed;
Half sunk,	stretch far away.
And wrinkled lip,	a shattered visage lies, whose frown,
Tell that its sculptor	from an antique land
. . . and so on	

To get this effect, without a lot of tedious work, use an unusual character such as the backslash (\ ) to mark where you want to break each line. Then select the lines, choose 'Convert text to Table', and when the dialogue box appears, tell Word that you want to break each line using the \ character. Voilà!

To mix one column up leaving the other one alone, select it, choose A–Z sort and click on the 'Options'. Tick the 'Sort column only' box. Now you can sort one column into alphabetical order while keeping the other in the right sequence.

Variations on this include splitting the lines into *three* columns, and mixing up the middles, or the two ends. In this way you can create puzzles of differentiated complexity and difficulty.

All of these kinds of activities work well using Word with an IWB and can be quickly prepared and stored. They work equally well on students' individual computers, working alone or in pairs. In most cases you will probably want to model the activity using the IWB, then allow time for students to work on their own (either with computers or on paper) and finally round off with a plenary: once again, use the IWB to bring together students' answers, suggestions and ideas, depending on the nature of the activity.

Preparation and resources

You will need a copy, in electronic form, of the text to be studied. If downloading texts from the Internet, see the Tip on p. xv of the Introduction.

Final words

If in the word sort activity you ask students to decide the categories themselves, what difference does it make? Try experimenting. Give one group fixed categories and leave another free to choose. What's the difference?

Chapter 8

Text-mapping

Using an IWB to map the verbal topography of a text, using emphasis tools and other markers

Text-mapping was invented by Tony Clifford as a way of exploiting the extraordinarily diverse marking effects available in a word processor:

Using Word, text can be

- bold
- italic
- underlined
- highlighted (15 colours)
- coloured (at least 40 colours)
- in a specific font
- a specific font size
- superscript or subscript.

The amazing thing is that at least seven of these effects can overlap on one word without obscuring legibility:

Still legible

The above word is simultaneously: bold, italic, underlined, highlighted yellow, red, Rockwell and 20 point and still be perfectly legible. The mapping, with all its visual impact, can be done in front of the class.

If you can mark text so well, you can assign meanings to each format or font effect. The classic routine is to write the key at the foot of the page – though we will be suggesting some other possibilities for this application. This is a versatile and adaptable technique that can be used for almost all on-screen text analysis and it is a core idea for text and the interactive whiteboard.

Lesson overview

Select a text that has a variety of interesting features (almost any text!).

Work on one text as a model for the class, discussing which words follow the same pattern, and for each pattern discuss what mark would be appropriate. Emphasis might be carried by font size – the more emphatic, the bigger the font; emotion carried by colour of font; underline/bold/italic assigned to word classes. You don't need to stick to existing classification schemes – this is one big chance to be inventive and for pupils to come up with their own meta-language to analyse the text. If someone says, 'There are lots of negatives in this text,' assign a marker to negatives. The only rule is that the key must refer to an objectively discernible pattern.

At this demo-stage, you can use extra text boxes and arrows to mark how the map is working on the screen. Once you are sure that everyone has grasped the principle, issue another text.

If they have access to their own computers, load a text on each machine and, with the class working in pairs or threes, ask them to map the text, recording their key at the foot of the document. Allow between 25 and 30 minutes (a shorter time if the exercise has become well practised) and then call each group to the front to present their maps, loading their work onto the whiteboard. You will be amazed at the richness of fresh insight and enthusiasm this exercise generates.

If they do not have access to computers, you can achieve some of the same effects with felt-tips and rulers, but the text will be degraded in the process and may become illegible. Unless you have something like a visualizer you will not be able easily to share the work with the rest of the class.

Example (opening paragraphs of *Bleak House*)

LONDON. Michaelmas Term lately over, and the Lord Chancellor sitting in Lincoln's Inn Hall. **Implacable** November weather. As much mud in the streets as if the waters had but newly retired from the face of the earth, and it would not be wonderful to meet a Megalosaurus, 40 feet long or so, waddling like an elephantine lizard up Holborn Hill. Smoke <u>lowering</u> down from chimney-pots, making a soft black drizzle, with **flakes of soot in it as big as full-grown snow-flakes** — gone into **mourning**, one might imagine, for the <u>death</u> <u>of the sun.</u> Dogs, <u>undistinguishable</u> in mire. Horses, scarcely better; splashed to their very <u>blinkers.</u> Foot passengers, **jostling** one another's umbrellas in a general **infection** of **ill-temper**, and losing their foot-hold at street-corners, where tens of thousands of other foot passengers have been slipping and sliding since the day broke (<u>if the day ever broke</u>), adding new deposits to the **crust upon crust of mud,** sticking at those points tenaciously to the pavement, and accumulating at compound interest.

Fog everywhere. Fog up the river, where it flows among green aits and meadows; fog down the river, where it rolls **defiled** among the tiers of shipping and the waterside **pollutions** of a great (and **dirty**) city. Fog on the Essex marshes, fog on the Kentish heights. Fog **creeping** into the cabooses of collier-brigs; fog lying out on the yards, and hovering in the rigging of great ships; fog drooping on the gunwales of barges and small boats. Fog in the eyes and throats of ancient Greenwich pensioners, **wheezing** by the firesides of their wards; fog in the stem and bowl of the afternoon pipe of the **wrathful** skipper, down in his close cabin; fog **cruelly pinching** the toes and fingers of his shivering little 'prentice boy on deck. Chance people on the bridges peeping over the parapets into a nether sky of fog, with fog all round them, as if they were up in a balloon, and hanging in the misty clouds

Key to text map:

Words with a heavy negative sense or implying bad temper

Words implying difficulty seeing

And so on . . .

Tips

- Use the same key to map two texts – for instance, the same news item taken from a tabloid and a broadsheet. The tracking of emotive terms can be fascinating!
- Choose texts that can be displayed on one screen (maximum about 300 words).
- Try text openings – the beginning of *Bleak House*, the opening lines of Keats' 'The Eve of St Agnes'; the first paragraph of *Nineteen Eighty-Four*. Authors attempting to establish scene very often use language in definite, vigorous ways to kick-start the narrative.

Using your IWB software instead of Word

All varieties of IWB software should prove useful for text-mapping. Most software won't allow Word-type highlighting, but to compensate, you have marker tools and pens. Arrows are great for an on-screen demo, but they look completely chaotic and get in the way of reading the text. Use page sorter view, and add as many new pages as there are items on your key. Use a fresh page for each key item and copy the target text onto each one. At the top of this key-page, write the definition (e.g. red text = feelings). Under the definition, brainstorm examples from the analysed text and the implications of the pattern that has been discovered.

Final words

The great thing is that the software allows you to jump instantly between the text being mapped and the individual key-pages. This is one of the most powerful features of using IWB – the ability to navigate around your material in an instant. You can even facilitate this process by inserting links into documents that take you from one page to another. Look up how to do it on your board and try out the idea.

Chapter 9

Gathering thoughts

There are many ways to organise thoughts on an individual level, but what works best with small *groups* or whole classes? The challenge is to make the whole activity explicit and easy to follow so that the discussion and thought processes contribute to a rich learning experience.

An IWB allows just such a high level of communal discussion and organisation – it can take an activity that has started at group level, perhaps with teams of thinkers working around a desk, and summarise the conclusions as a whole-class activity, pulling the strands together and making the conclusions public.

Working with conventional classroom materials, a typical lesson might involve jotting down ideas, ranking, clustering, contrasting them, and then drawing connections between connected concepts to create spider diagrams. Concept-mapping or mind-mapping programs attempt to replicate these processes in electronic form – with the advantage that each stage can be saved and everything can be edited.

If you don't want to start the adventure of concept-mapping, or you feel daunted by the complexity of the associated software, there are many ways that an IWB can be harnessed to bring thoughts together or to stimulate discussion, and most of them can work without specialist software. You just need to know what you want and adapt the programs you already have for the purpose.

On the simplest level, to work effectively, you need a method of disaggregating information – the digital equivalent of cutting up a piece of paper into cards. You also need a way of moving the resultant fragments (often called 'tiles' or 'fridge magnets') around your IWB, colouring and marking them as necessary. Tiles can carry words or pictures. For instance you could use a stack of suitable image cards to start the chapter 'Investigating symbols'.

Once you have made your cards, think about the 'background' – the diagram or shape that will give enhanced meaning when the class is organising the tiles. Simple quadrants, Venn diagrams or tables are perfectly adequate, and will allow you to develop quite sophisticated patterns of thought and connection.

LESSON IDEAS

In Word, divide the screen into four quadrants. You could use a table with two columns and two rows. Press 'Enter' repeatedly to make your cells square-shaped. You can use colour fills if you wish to make the whole effect eye-catching. You could use symbolic colours, progressing from green = positive to red = negative with two intermediate states represented by yellow and orange, or simply label each quadrant.

Next, make some tiles using text boxes. These can contain text, or you can insert a picture into them. Stack them up in the centre of the diagram ready for use. Save the result. To create multiple empty tiles using Word, create one text box tile, select it, right-click and choose 'Copy'. Now if you repeatedly 'Paste' (click in free space between each 'Paste') you will make lots of tiles – all you need to do is drag words from a text into the tiles. Tedious, I know, but you can save the results of your labours and use them again and again for different classes. (The shortcut for copy is Ctrl+C, and for paste it is Ctrl+V.)

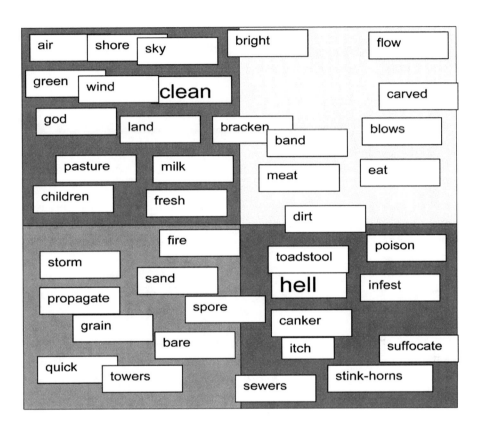

Here I've borrowed the words from a poem, 'Windscale' by Norman Nicholson, first discarding duplicates and the so-called grammatical words (prepositions, pronouns, articles) – with the challenge of sorting the words from positive to negative. Each word coming off the stack elicits its own discussion.

Now, having sorted the tiles roughly from positive to negative, ask which word is most positive. Re-size it accordingly by dragging the edge of the tile. You can make the text in some tiles bold or italic, assigning a meaning to these – or change the tile background colour.

When students finally encounter the poem itself, they will already be sensitive to the implicit positive/negative polarisation of the text, and their ability to 'read' it will have been significantly enhanced. This enriches understanding straight away.

Quadrants such as this can be also used for a form of instant self-assessment. Create a set of tiles with your students' names on them. Students come to the front and move their names to the quadrant that best represents their level of confidence with the topic about to be addressed. Save this screen. After the lesson, display the same screen and ask students to move their names if they feel they have progressed. Re-sizing names can also represent levels of enthusiasm or enjoyment.

In a similar way you can write a proposition across the centre of the square and arrange tiles in relationship to it.

For instance, create three versions of the board entitled 'The Reputation Index', with these propositions:

- 'At the beginning of the play, Macbeth . . .'
- 'In the middle of the play, Macbeth . . .'
- 'At the end of the play, Macbeth . . .'

Create a set of tiles with the play's main characters' names on them and drag them into position to show whether they have a positive or negative reputation. Variations could include 'The Loyalty Index' showing characters loyal to Macbeth.

If you want to experiment with images, why not try gathering a collection of pictures from Google Images showing the roles of men and women in society – then, through discussion, group each image along the continuum positive/negative.

If you find success with simple quadrants, try Venn diagrams and other diagrams. Once you have grasped the idea and practised the classroom organisation required for an efficient lesson, you will discover how powerful and engaging this technique can be, open to a very wide range applications.

Finding programs to support this approach is not difficult; some you might have already, which can be adapted for this purpose; others, specially designed for the task, you will need to track down, and some of these you may need to pay for. Here are some starting points:

- Smart Notebook software enables you to write information onto tiles and drag, re-size, rotate and colour it. It won't split up a text for you, so you have to do the disaggregation by hand.
- Promethean Flipcharts offer similar facilities.
- MS Word has text boxes, as discussed on p. 48. These can be awkward to use in a class-teaching context, but, as shown, you can make draggable cards that will re-size and colour. Again, the software won't split up a text for you, so you have to do the disaggregation by hand, piece by piece.

- Teachit's Magnet – one of the best paid-for resources – allows you to make sophisticated *flippable* tiles (you can store information on the backs of tiles and flip them over to show it). Paste a text into the window and the program will automatically chop it up for you, but you cannot rotate the resulting tiles. It comes with some ready-made backgrounds.
- Triptico's Word Magnets Plus is a very easy program to use 'out of the box'. It allows dragging, rotating, re-sizing and colouring. Paste a text into the window and the program will automatically chop it up for you. The tiles can carry images too. Usefully, it comes with 42 of the organisational background diagrams, ready-made. Nice!
- Websites such as *Cool Tools for Schools* (http://cooltoolsforschools.wiki spaces.com/Organiser+Tools) will give you links to a bewildering variety of presentation and thought-organisation programs. Explore (if you have the time) and experiment to find your favourite.

Your IWB

Explore the resources you get with your own IWB. Look for backgrounds. If there aren't any supplied ready-made, consider creating a set. Templates for some of these can be found stored in Word. Go to 'Insert' and select 'Diagram'.

Final words

Because you have the central focus of the class with an IWB, organising thoughts and ideas, brainstorming and mind-mapping are all facilitated. Used sparingly, you will find these activities generate a high level of mental stimulation.

Chapter 10

Collapsing and re-sorting texts

A collapsed or 'alphabetised' text is a poem or passage of prose in which the words have been rearranged into alphabetical order. (There are variations on this, such as 'rhyme sort', or reversed sorting or listings that omit duplicates.) The result is a cluster of vocabulary that reflects the nature of the original text, but not its composed meaning. We can use these lists to make informed guesses about the original text, or to use its lexical choices for new creative work.

Collapsing and re-sorting text is an effective way to hide the meaning of the original text while providing plenty of clues as to its spirit, principal subject and tone. The form and the argument of the text are obscured, focusing attention on the choice of words. This makes discussion of the text – once revealed – more meaningful and informed.

A collapsed text can be prepared quickly and efficiently using Word.

1   Make sure it is a 'clean' text – that is, scanned or typed. If you copy and paste from a web page, take care. Some texts bring with them 'embedded' information which can prevent things working as you expect. See the Tip in Chapter 5.
2   Go to 'Replace' in the 'Edit' menu (Word 2003) or in the 'Home' menu (Word 2010) or hold down Ctrl and tap the letter 'H'.

> Type a space in the 'Find what:' box
> Type ^p in the 'Replace with:' box (NB: a lower-case p)
> Click on 'Replace All'. This should put the text into a long thin line.

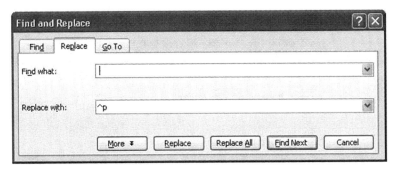

3   Go to 'Table > Sort' (2003) or select 'Sort ⬆⬇' in the 'Home' menu (2010).
    Click 'OK' (ignore other options!) and this should sort it alphabetically.
4   Go back to 'Replace'

> Type ^p in the 'Find what:' box. Make sure you have deleted the space you typed earlier.
> Type a space in the 'Replace with:' box.
> Click on 'Replace All'.
> This should put it back into a paragraph like the example on p. 55.

5   You can use Format > Change case (2003) or the 'Change Case' icon Aa˅ in the 'Home' menu (2010) to put it all in lower case if you wish. Use Find and Replace to remove full stops, commas, and so on. Save your fridge magnets with a new filename

> Problems? The most likely causes of it not working are that at stage 4 you left a space in the 'Find what:' box next to the ^p. Spaces are small and invisible, so just check. Alternatively, you may have inadvertently selected a part of the document somewhere and the program is applying your instructions just to that one bit. Make sure none of your text is selected, or that *all* of it is.

LESSON IDEAS

I. What kind of text?

Using the collapsed text technique, a whole class can engage interactively with a passage and explore what kind of text it might be rather than applying sterile rules.

Pick out interesting language features and mark them in different ways of your choice. Once unfamiliar or unusual words have been examined, you might move on to looking at what word classes are prominent or absent. In this example, there are many adjectives and nouns, fewer verbs and no pronouns. This on its own makes narrative an impossibility. Out of context, it is also difficult to tell some adjectives and nouns apart, and this is a good moment to revise the way in which words can take on different roles in a sentence.

What kind of writing tends to have this sort of ratio of word classes? The answer is a certain kind of descriptive writing where space is at a premium

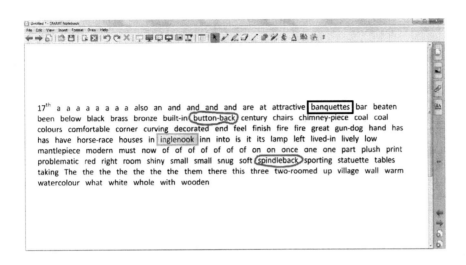

17th a a a a a a a a also an and and and and are at attractive banquettes bar beaten been below black brass bronze built-in button-back century chairs chimney-piece coal coal colours comfortable corner curving decorated end feel finish fire fire great gun-dog hand has has have horse-race houses in inglenook inn into is it its lamp left lived-in lively low mantlepiece modern must now of of of of of of on on once one one part plush print problematic red right room shiny small small snug soft spindleback sporting statuette tables taking The the the the the the the them there this three two-roomed up village wall warm watercolour what white whole with wooden

and every word must count. This is the world of guides and brochures, where a lot has to be condensed into a small space – in this case, *The Good Pub Guide*.

2. Word classes

While we are on the topic of word classes or 'parts of speech', the kind of text we're looking at can be the subject of a formal analysis. This is best done using Word rather than IWB software. Project the text in question onto the whiteboard and, using drag and drop, move words into categories. Pupils can come and take charge if they wish; the kinetic element makes an otherwise rather mechanical activity much more engaging.

In this example, taken from a brochure for a tourist attraction in North Wales, we are focusing on words which could fulfil a dual role and suggesting contexts for them. Once the kind of text is revealed, pupils will spot that 'parking', for example, is far more likely to be used as a noun than a verb and 'adventure' as an adjective rather than a noun, especially as 'playground' also appears. The paucity of verbs will gradually become apparent too – typical of a bullet-point list.

*and and and and and and and audio aviary birds breathtaking bring
butterflies café gifts centre discovery events exhibitions first free free from
gallery games garden shome infinity inventions junction just maze national of
of off on parkland parlour peaceful picnic playground popular portrait science
souvenirs special story terrace the the the the the the the tour training
trenches views walk walled war Welsh with woodland world yesteryear your*

Nouns	Adjectives	Verbs
adventure	adventure	
	amazing	amazing
parking		parking
	rolling	rolling

3. Fridge magnet fun

This activity is really a spin-off and is best demonstrated on the whiteboard and then carried out by pupils on their own computers, or even on paper if that is all that is available. Collapse a text, say a poem, and display it using Word. Remind them of the qualities possessed by fridge magnets and that they are going to create some pieces of writing using just the words provided. Model the kind of thing you want them to attempt, just creating some interesting-sounding phrases. Don't imply that you want them to write in full sentences or to create a poem, though the latter may often be the outcome.

If these are the fridge magnets supplied:

a an ancient and are ashore Atlantic baby beach black blue box breakers broomstick Chinese colour corners cowboy dinosaurs dragon electric fifth fire first fish from gold great high-rolling hinges horse I ice in is its joints joke last leaping lid man my night nostrils of on put rumbling sari season secrets shall silk sip smile snow spark spoken stars steel summer sun surf swish the then three toe tongue tooth top touching uncle violet wash water white wild wishes witch with yellow

you might make a few phrases like this:

ancient dinosaurs smile

the leaping dragon jokes

and electric secrets spark

And, yes, we have allowed an 's' to be added to joke. Changes of tense or number to allow agreement are to be welcomed!

Tips

- While the ICT route is neater than the paper-scissors-cards approach, you may want to try combinations. Cards have specific uses – they're tactile and encourage group discussions. Perhaps launch the lesson with the IWB, try a card-sort exercise with a limited number of words, and end back on the IWB for summary and discussion.
- A card-based version of the same exercise would also be useful if you want to mix the class activity by spending part of the lesson working in groups round tables.

Chapter 11

Exploring text types

Using the IWB to analyse text types

A powerful alternative application of the collapsed text approach is to offer students texts that come from a wide range of text types. Is it possible to isolate the key words, and the key patterns of repetition, that identify text types? Does it work even when the text has been re-sorted into alphabetical or random order?

The analytical procedure can be demonstrated in a plenary involving the whole class; the class can then split into pairs to work on paper-based resources, or files on individual computers.

Lesson overview

The lesson begins with a display of some text types in collapsed form. The class examines each example – spotting key vocabulary items and marking them, noting especially prominent or interesting repetitions, deducing as much as they can from the form of verbs and so on.

On the IWB the process can be enhanced by:

- highlighting words
- clustering like terms in one part of the screen
- using the Flipchart or Notebook facility to write a commentary and record deductions and suggestions.

The lesson then proceeds to individual work.

If the class has access to computers, make sure the working file is available on the shared part of the network. Students mark the word lists and fill in the commentary sections of the table, extending and developing lines of thought introduced in the plenary. If there's time, these modified files can be displayed to the whole class to conclude the lesson, with a spoken commentary provided by the team doing the analysis.

If they do not have access to computers, the class can work on print-outs of the sheets, recording thoughts and underlining text in longhand.

Conclude the lesson by showing the original text and illustrating the patterns in that context.

Preparation and resources

The key to the success of this activity is to choose texts with distinctive features:

- a Shakespeare sonnet or a passage from a play
- a short extract from a novel
- modern poetry
- a bit from a Harry Potter novel that doesn't include any give-away names
- adverts
- a recipe
- short newspaper articles
- a menu
- a horoscope
- travel writing.

Gathering the texts may be quite hard work. Converting them to collapsed versions is relatively straightforward, especially if you use an online application to do the work for you (for instance, Teachit's Cruncher).

Example

Here is a sample of texts arranged in a suitable table format:

Text for analysis	*Commentary*
T1	
a a a adventures ancient and are are are breathtaking craggy dreamed earth from inspire land leave many middle mists mountain mythical of of only own peaks place spells step stories story take the this to told track vistas welcome well-worn where where will with woven you your your	
T2	
a a a airborne and and and and and and becomes bills CO2 construction conversion deck disruptive dust dusty expensive far go heating in insulates less loft loft moisture one out perfect pollution re-roof reduces reduces roof seals seals sound stabilises start than to warm wet whole windy	

T3	
0–60km 2900km 5500°c a a a also and and and and and approximately are beginning between but called carries carries centre continental core core core core core core core crust crust crust crust crust diameter different down earth earth earth earth earth energy engine extremely hard has heat here hot hottest immense in in inner inner inner inner inner inner iron iron is is is is is is is is is is is is is it it it it it its land layer layer layer layer layer like liquid live lower made made made magma mantle mantle mantle melt nearer nickel nickel oceanic of of of of of of of of of of of outer outer part parts rock rock rock rock room section semi-molten similar soft solid solid still surrounding temperatures temperatures the the the the the the the the the the the the the the the the the the the the the the the the the the the the there thick thin to to to two types up up up up upon upper water we which which which widest with with with	

Tips

- When displaying these texts, use the biggest font that will fit comfortably in the window.
- Experiment with the other forms of collapsed text (one that eliminates duplicates; one that 'rhyme-sorts' the text, for instance).
- Apply the idea to genre work.

Your IWB

If you use Smart Notebook to display the collapsed text, you can disaggregate the text simply by dragging each word out of the text box, effectively giving it a text box of its own: tedious, but effective. Word will suffice quite well otherwise!

All major IWBs will allow you to annotate and comment, and save your comments as you proceed.

Final words

We invented collapsing a text as a classroom technique in 1998 – to our delight, it's become widespread.

Chapter 12

One thing after another

Sequencing

Young people love puzzles, and one of the most effective ways to encourage students to look closely at a text is to turn it into a puzzle. You will find other examples of this approach in this book!

A de-sequenced text is just such a puzzle. However, this is an activity which is difficult to carry out using traditional means such as cutting up small slips of paper. There is something satisfying about moving pieces of text on card, of course, but making them is time-consuming and certainly not something you can do in five minutes or less before the start of a lesson.

ICT offers a straightforward solution to this problem and is a way of creating almost instant lessons which can focus on language, textual cohesion, text types and the study of literature – and probably much more.

LESSON IDEAS

1. Blank verse

The focus of the lesson is the structure of a piece of blank verse. First, introduce the students to the poem and talk about the nature of blank verse. Once these building blocks are established, introduce the de-sequenced version and have the students help to put it back into the right order.

Take the closing lines from Tennyson's 'Ulysses' and de-sequence the text. The quickest way to do this is in Word. Select the text you wish to de-sequence and then click on the alphabetical sort option: ↕ (to be found in the 'Table' menu in Word 2003 or in the 'Home' tab in the newer versions of Word). The lines will be sorted in alphabetical order of the first letter of the line:

And see the great Achilles, whom we knew

Come, my friends,

It may be that the gulfs will wash us down:

It may be we shall touch the Happy Isles,

Made weak by time and fate, but strong in will

Moved earth and heaven; that which we are, we are;

Of all the western stars, until I die.

One equal temper of heroic hearts,

Push off, and sitting well in order smite

The sounding furrows; for my purpose holds

Though much is taken, much abides; and though

'Tis not too late to seek a newer world.

To sail beyond the sunset, and the baths

To strive, to seek, to find, and not to yield.

We are not now that strength which in old days

The lines can be moved using the IWB, the on-screen keyboard, or the computer mouse or keyboard. If using the IWB directly, the easiest way is to click in the margin so that a single line is selected and then drag the line to wherever you wish. If pupils are sufficiently adept (and tall), they can do this themselves. A simple method using your computer keyboard is to position your cursor within the line to be moved (no need to select it) and use the keys Shift, Alt and up or down arrows. This gives very precise control and is well worth explaining to pupils so that they can use the same method when working on their own.

While the puzzle is being studied, take suggestions from pupils and use various forms of emphasis (highlighter, bold, italic, fonts, etc.) to mark, for example:

- where there is a continuation implied
- where there is a halt
- suggestions where they see a link between two lines.

They may also wish to note

- words or phrases with a significance regarding the form or style of the poem, e.g. 'my friends'
- words or phrases which are interesting or archaic, e.g. 'smite'
- in rhyming poetry, the rhyme scheme.

Using suggestions from the pupils, move lines both when a link has been established and when you wish to try out a connection. Trial and error (iterative learning) is impotant, and ICT lends itself to this approach.

2. Prose in rows

Re-sequencing also works with prose but with slight modifications. Decide whether you wish to organise your text by lines, sentences or paragraphs. If you wish to work with a lengthy text, de- and re-sequencing by paragraph is probably the best option, provided these are not too long. Analysing the paragraph order of a text is a good way of looking at how articles and essays (including the students' own) can be structured in a logical manner.

If you wish to examine a shorter text in more detail, it can be done by sentence or by line, but in either case you will have to insert line breaks (using the Enter key) at the end of lines or a sentences in order to move them smoothly.

For example, arranged by sentence:

- In telling these stories, Jane Austen takes the opportunity to create many carefully observed characters.
- Jane Austen's stories are more concerned with people than action.
- She is especially good at showing someone's character through their conversation.
- The path of love never runs smoothly and there are usually many difficulties and misunderstandings in the way of the couple.
- The plots centre on the romantic ups and downs of heroines, who in the end are happily married to the hero.
- You can see this, for example, in the way that Isabella and her brother John, speak.

Arranged by line, the passage appears like this:

- conversation. You can see this, for example, in the way that Isabella and her brother John, speak.
- couple. In telling these stories, Jane Austen takes the opportunity to create many carefully
- Jane Austen's stories are more concerned with people than action. The plots centre on the romantic
- observed characters. She is specially good at showing someone's character through their
- runs smoothly and there are usually many difficulties and misunderstandings in the way of the
- ups and downs of heroines, who in the end are happily married to the hero. The path of love never

The former probably makes more sense, but the latter is easier to solve. Over to you!

Once you have tried sequencing, you will find many situations in which it is useful. It is a challenging exercise for the more able as well as an excellent revision tool. Furthermore, the approach takes moments to prepare, which makes it ideal for a cover lesson (even for another subject area) or when you simply haven't had time to do all the preparation that you would have liked.

Tips

- Stop whenever you feel the task is no longer paying dividends. You do not have to persevere until every line is correct. Display the original and check where your version is correct and where it is not. Examine why some lines are hard to place; this is not necessarily a lack of understanding – the text may have more than one way of making sense!

If students have access to their own computers, they can repeat the activity in pairs or individually: an invaluable revision exercise. They could then tackle a different extract. As a plenary, the class will then be well placed to re-order the text using the whiteboard, with you bringing out aspects of structure and meaning which assist the re-sequencing.

If students do not have access to their own computers, they can be given print-outs, together with a new text to work on. Having studied these and marked them in any way that is helpful, they then feed back to the class as the texts are re-ordered, perhaps using a timer to see how quickly it can be done.

Try this yourself with some poems with which you are only partly familiar. Not only is this good for your own brain, but it will help you to model problem-solving techniques as you go along. It's also good for the students to understand that you don't always know all the answers *but* you have strategies to help you when you're stuck!

Chapter 13

Making notes is hard to do

One of the skills which students are expected to master as they pass through secondary education is that of note-taking, yet it is rarely taught as a specific skill. Perhaps this is because it is a very difficult thing to teach. On the surface, making a note of what is important and leaving out the rest would seem to be the simplest of tasks. In reality, students find it very hard, frequently collecting far too much information and failing to summarise what they have gleaned.

While the use of ICT and an interactive whiteboard will not solve these problems, they do offer an alternative approach which is very straightforward. The approach relies on a facility in Word which allows you to mark certain words and phrases (e.g. by highlighting them) and then delete the remaining text. For example, take a short extract from which we decide to keep only the nouns, which we highlight using the highlighter tool:

> A picturesque pleasure park providing visitors with 'living pictures', including a cascade, a waterwheel, a Temple of Bacchus, a Gothic tower, a triumphal Roman arch, and a ruined abbey, among other fanciful follies.

A series of key strokes will remove the non-highlighted words, leaving:

> park visitors pictures' cascade waterwheel Temple tower arch abbey follies

which can, if wished, be arranged in a list.

The technique uses the 'Find and Replace' function, as follows. Take a passage of your choice and highlight some words or phrases. Now open the 'Find and Replace' dialogue box and click on 'More'. The box doubles in size (and More changes to Less). The cursor should be in the upper ('Find what:') area.

Click on 'Format' at the bottom of the dialogue box and select 'Highlight' from the drop-down menu:

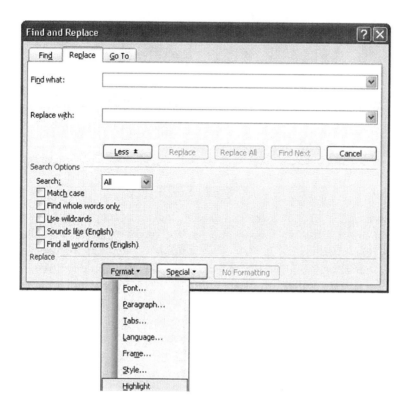

The word 'Highlight' will now appear under the writeable area. Now click 'Highlight' *again* from the drop-down menu. 'Not highlight' should appear under the 'Find what:' writeable area.

Click into the 'Replace with:' writable area and type a space (which you won't see) or use a marker such as / or ^p. The former two will just separate the highlighted words or phrases with a space or forward slash; the latter will put each one on a new line. You choose.

Click on 'Replace All', and 'OK'. All the non-highlighted text will disappear, leaving you with just your selected words.

Tip

- It's a good idea to have another version of your text saved somewhere else . . .

LESSON IDEAS

I. Gathering the main points from a non-fiction text

Select a text from which you wish to gather the main points. For example:

> Bellevue Manor has made a successful start in the Borders in Bloom awards this year, earning a Silver award.
>
> It was described by the judging panel as 'a beautiful quiet space in the middle of a busy town' and the team of volunteers who maintain the garden are delighted with their success.
>
> John de Vere, head gardener at Bellevue Manor, who manages the team, said:
>
> 'We're all excited with the Silver award. We feel that the garden is one of Craigton's best kept secrets. We hope that this recognition will encourage people to discover this wonderful garden, almost hidden behind the Old School and Almshouses.'
>
> The judges commended the environmental approach taken in the garden. As John explained: 'We are very much an organic site and at all times we use hand tools instead of power tools. Wildlife is encouraged and we use produce from the garden in our restaurant, including anything from parsley to pears on the menu.'
>
> The judges were impressed not only by the carefully maintained appearance of the garden, but also by the fact that it is well used. It is enjoyed by visitors to the house and is also a place where many functions, including weddings and civic receptions, are held.

Display the text on the whiteboard and use the highlighter tool to pick out the most significant phrases. You may wish to distribute the passage on paper and ask students to do the same thing with highlighter pens, working in pairs. Then you will be able to gather their ideas and comment on them as you proceed. Here is one possible selection:

> Bellevue Manor has made a successful start in the Borders in Bloom awards this year, earning a Silver award.
>
> It was described by the judging panel as 'a beautiful quiet space in the middle of a busy town' and the team of volunteers who maintain the garden are delighted with their success.
>
> John de Vere, head gardener at Bellevue Manor, who manages the team, said:

'We're all excited with the Silver award. We feel that the garden is one of Craigton's best kept secrets. We hope that this recognition will encourage people to discover this wonderful garden, almost hidden behind the Old School and Almshouses.'

The judges commended the environmental approach taken in the garden. As John explained: 'We are very much an organic site and at all times we use hand tools instead of power tools. Wildlife is encouraged and we use produce from the garden in our restaurant, including anything from parsley to pears on the menu.'

The judges were impressed not only by the carefully maintained appearance of the garden, but also by the fact that it is well used. It is enjoyed by visitors to the house and is also a place where many functions, including weddings and civic receptions, are held.

Point out where repetition has been avoided in the selection and examples kept to a minimum. Stripped of the unselected text, the result is:

Bellevue Manor / Borders in Bloom awards / earning / Silver / judging panel / beautiful quiet space / volunteers / delighted / John de Vere, head gardener / one of Craigton's best kept secrets / encourage / people / to discover this wonderful garden / judges / commended the environmental approach / organic site / use hand tools / Wildlife / encouraged / produce from the garden in our restaurant / judges / impressed / carefully maintained appearance / well used / functions / are held

You can then work on improving these rough notes into something more readable – but still in note form. Use Word or your whiteboard software to arrange and edit what you have distilled. Point out that similar phrases can be grouped together, such as the opinions of the judges.

Bellevue Manor has earned Silver in Borders in Bloom awards

Judging panel said: beautiful quiet space; commended the environmental approach; impressed by carefully maintained appearance; and that it is well used; many functions held there

Volunteers delighted. John de Vere, head gardener, said: one of Craigton's best kept secrets, will encourage people to discover it; organic site: use hand tools, encourage wildlife, use produce from garden in restaurant

Students should now be shown how to use the technique themselves and try their hands at a different passage. Paper and highlighter will come in useful when no computer access is possible but it is important that they experience this quick and satisfying method first, if at all possible.

2. Find that poem!

The same technique can be used to create found poems. Take a piece of writing which contains some powerful description or interesting use of imagery and display it to the class. Give them a few minutes to read it and make a note (mental or written) of phrases they particularly like. Take feedback from the class and mark with the highlighter tool a good selection of suggestions. This example is taken from a description by a Y9 student:

> My cat is as vain as a film star or a queen like Cleopatra. She purrs like she has an engine deep down in her throat or her chest and her evil green eyes shine in her face like emeralds. She meows pathetically and gets ignored or fed. But later behind her half-closed eyelids she dribbles in contentment. She sleeps all day, lazy as a cow but I suppose she's as gentle and as graceful as a ballerina when she wants to be. When she walks along the wall it's as if she's a tightrope walker on padded paws. When she's asleep she's just like any other furry fat cat.

The selected phrases are retained and the rest deleted.

vain as a film star

purrs like she has an engine deep down in her throat

evil green eyes shine in her face like emeralds

she dribbles in contentment.

lazy as a cow

graceful as a ballerina

furry fat cat

Some sensitive editing will produce a satisfying result which students will recognise as a poem, though they may not be able to say why. This is an opportunity to talk about poetry often being the most compressed form of writing, retaining only the best and most essential words . . .

My cat
vain as a film star
she purrs like she has an engine
deep down in her throat
her evil green eyes
shine in her face like emeralds
she dribbles in contentment
lazy as a cow
but graceful as a ballerina –
furry fat cat

Tips

- Don't tell the class that they are going to create a poem – let it emerge.
- Effective results can be obtained from all sorts of texts, including recipe books and travel writing. Try it yourself!

Chapter 14

Word bits

Interactive whiteboards are both visual and kinaesthetic. This can be very useful for students who find concentrating on words on a page less than stimulating. These students may also be the ones who have yet to internalise some of the basics of spelling and word-building.

One approach is to take longer words and break them down into constituent parts, or to see which words can be found using consecutive letters within longer words. This could be done using Word but the software provided with your IWB tends to be more user-friendly for this kind of activity. If you make sure your text is 'live' – that is, in text-editing mode – then you can simply drag and drop your word bits anywhere on the page.

LESSON IDEAS

1. Breaking up is good to do

Decide on your list of words and then type or paste them onto your whiteboard. One per page is probably a good idea.

Model the process by selecting a part of the word and then dragging it to another part of the page. Ask students to come and do the same thing with other words they recognise. Guide them if necessary by giving clues.

You could choose a selection of compound words such as snowman, bookshelf, football or whiteboard. Drag out the constituent words. There may be some that you don't spot – sometimes the smallest, like he or elf.

For fun, rather than as an academic exercise, see if they can come up with a sentence or short paragraph which uses all of the words. It doesn't matter that a word like bookshelf has relatively few words in it – it's the activity of finding them that is likely to impress itself on the users.

book

he

bookshelf

she

elf

shelf

You may wish to arrange them in a way that reinforces the pattern of the words.

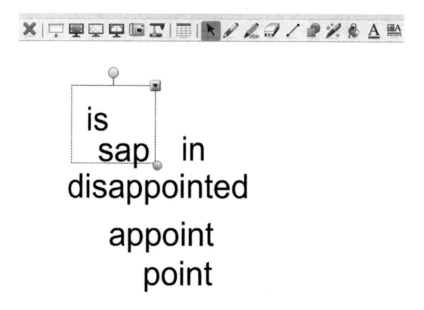

Use a similar approach to look at suffixes and prefixes or, as a variation, have the suffixes or prefixes available to be added to the stems where appropriate.

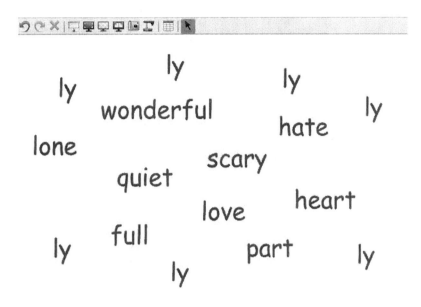

2. Mnemonics

A development of this approach is to use the functions of the IWB software, or simply Word, to bring out aspects of hard-to-spell words which might help students to remember their structure. This is very much a personal thing, but for many people a visual reminder will work better than a complicated verbal rationale.

For example, accentuate the science in conscience and relate it to conscious.

con<u>science</u>

con<u>sci</u>ous

Or play around with the way a word is displayed:

*acc*ommodate

av*ail*able

med*ici*ne

These look impressive displayed on the whiteboard, and much experimentation can take place as the class comes to an agreement that such and such an arrangement is the best. Later they can create their own – a great way for them to learn spellings as well as providing some interesting wall displays.

Tips

- Any words that are difficult to spell can be used – the chin in machinery or the sin in business may prove to be a useful mnemonic for some students.
- This does not have to be a major part of a lesson. It could be a technique you use when a difficult word comes up in the course of a lesson. All you need is a selection of words and the time to paste them into your whiteboard page.
- In either Smart Notebook or Promethean Flipchart, a selected word, part-word or phrase (when dragged somewhere else on the page) will be copied rather than cut, which is very convenient.

Chapter 15

A 'stand-out' lesson!

Foregrounding key elements of a text

Word has a number of very clever tricks hidden in its mass of options. Some of these were intended by the software designers; some come about through the subversion of the software, producing effects never imagined by the program makers. We like to call these features 'conjuring tricks', because once you've mastered the sleight of hand required, the effects can appear quite magical.

If you want to lift a word from a text and animate it 'on the fly', select it, then hold down Ctrl and press the right square bracket key]. The text will grow by one point size. If you hold the two keys down, a beautiful smooth animation will take place – neatly foregrounding the text you want to highlight for the class's attention.

To make the text revert to its original size, hold down Ctrl and press the other square bracket – or alternatively hold down the Ctrl+Z key or use the Undo button – and everything will go into reverse.

Try this – hold down Ctrl and double-click on the verbs in a text on the screen. They will each be selected. Keep holding down Ctrl and press the square bracket to make the words mushroom in size.

O, if I wake, shall I not be distraught,
Environed with all these hideous fears?
And madly play with my forefather's joints?
And pluck the mangled Tybalt from his shroud?
And, in this rage, with some great kinsman's bone,
As with a club, dash out my desperate brains?
O, look! methinks I see my cousin's ghost
Seeking out Romeo, that did spit his body
Upon a rapier's point: stay, Tybalt, stay!
Romeo, I come! this do I drink to thee.

While the words are all still selected, you can make them bold, or click on the highlighter icon to make them stand out even more – all instant effects, visually eye-catching and a powerful way to emphasise a learning point.

Another way in Word to enlarge the whole text currently on the screen is to hold down Ctrl and rotate the wheel in the centre of your mouse (if you have one). This alters the zoom level – each click of wheel equals 10 per cent – and you can make one paragraph instantly fill the whole screen without altering the format. This is another good foregrounding technique to remember, and also essential if you want to make text legible to the whole class.

Found poems 'discovered' in an extended text

There are many more similar effects. Here's a good recipe for found poems – poems that occur by chance in an existing text. Traditionally these were marked by obscuring the unwanted words with heavy felt-tip pens. This technique again uses Word's 'Replace' function (hold down Ctrl and press H).

In the example below we have used the trick to print a typical 'found' poem. It swiftly foregrounds the target words and drops the rest into background grey!

Macbeth, Act I, Scene VII.

Mach. If it were done when 'tis done, then 'twere well

It were done quickly; if **the assassination**

Could trammel up the consequence, and catch

With his surcease success; that but this blow

Might be the be-all and the end-all here,

But here, upon this bank and shoal of time,

We'd jump the life to come. But in these cases

We still have judgment here; that we but teach

Bloody instructions, which, being taught, return

To plague the inventor; this even-handed justice

Commends the ingredients of our poison'd chalice

To our own lips. He's here in double trust:

First, as **I am** his kinsman and his subject,

Strong both against the deed; then, as his host,

Who should against **his murderer** shut the door,

Not bear **the knife** myself. Besides, this Duncan

Hath borne his faculties so meek, hath been

So clear **in his** great office, that his virtues

Will plead like angels trumpet-tongu'd against

The deep damnation of his taking-off;

And pity, like a **naked** new-born babe,

Striding the blast, or heaven's cherubin, hors'd

Upon the sightless couriers of the air,

Shall blow the horrid deed in every eye,

That tears shall drown the wind. I have no spur

To prick the **sides** of my intent, but only

Vaulting ambition, which o'er-leaps itself

And falls on the other.——

This is how to achieve the effect very swiftly:

- First get the text – simply lift it off the Internet – and open it in Word. If you find it comes accompanied by unwanted formatting, try copying it into the Windows Accessory program, Notepad, and then copying it again into Word – a technique that effectively disinfects the text of hidden controls.
- Highlight the words you have 'found' to make your found poem, using the highlighter tool on the menu bar: it looks like a pen. (After you have selected highlighter, the mouse pointer appears as a highlighter pen when you hover over the text.) Simply double-click on your chosen words.
- Select 'Replace' by holding down Ctrl and pressing H.
- You will see a simple menu initially. Click on 'More' to see an expanded version of the menu. You are looking for 'Format', because what we'll be doing is replacing the format but leaving the words unchanged.
- First click in the 'Find what:' box. Now click on 'Format' at the foot of the box and choose 'Highlight'.
- You can see the word 'Highlight' now appears just under the 'Find what:' box.
- Click in the 'Replace with:' box (*don't forget this step!*) and again click on 'Format'. This time choose 'Font'.
- You will see a box of options appear on. Select a big font size, an alternative colour (color!) and even another font.

- Now all you have to do is click on 'Replace All', and hey presto! The chosen words stand out beautifully.

This seems a complicated routine, but in reality takes a matter of seconds to perform.

It has the effect of enlarging and colouring the text you have selected as your found poem.

To grey out the surrounding text, first get rid of the 'Find and Replace' information already in the dialogue box by clicking on each box and selecting 'No Formatting'.

Click in the 'Find what:' box and select 'Highlight', as above. Now do it again *a second time*. You'll see the option change, magically, to 'Not highlight' – in other words, the computer will find all the words that haven't been highlighted.

In the 'Replace with:' box choose font colour grey, by selecting 'Format', 'Font' and then 'Color' (US spelling!) and choosing grey (usually at the bottom of the list of colours, so keep scrolling till you see it).

Click 'Replace All'.

It's worth persevering with this technique. Puzzle over it and work out the logic of it.

Replace can be a powerful ally in a whole host of language operations, and can help you mark or map a text, as in this example.

A moment's reflection will give you a host of applications for creative work in English:

- Prepare texts before a lesson to investigate the functions of certain words.
- Show pupils the technique and allow them to map their own texts.
- Encourage pupils to 'discover' found poems in other texts.

More found poems – creating poems in the style of Edwin Morgan

Edwin Morgan's experimental, playful approach to words and ideas matches perfectly with the fluidity and flexibility of a word processor. You can move words around and experiment to your heart's content. We're going to look at one special poem: 'Message Clear' (http://edwinmorgan.scottishpoetrylibrary. org.uk/poems/message_clear.html).

This poem 'finds' a poem in the biblical text 'I am the resurrection and the life'. It got us thinking – what other poems could be 'found' in the same way in other phrases, and how could the computer make such discoveries painless and effective?

Usually one 'discovers' a poem in a text by isolating whole words in it, in sequence, making those words say something interesting. 'Message Clear' goes one step further. It finds words in the *letters* of the target statement:

- spelt in sequence
- spelt correctly.

Once you know the rules, it is possible (as in the game Boggle, but with even more restrictions) to isolate all the possible words in a given phrase. When you've done that (a wonderful end-of-term exercise because it has a creative payload), you can try to form a meaningful sequence from words in the list – and there you have it, an Edwin Morgan found poem!

Let's look at an example: 'William Shakespeare'. How many words can be found in the great man's name?

Simply working through, letter by letter, try to spot as many words you can. Here's the result. Some are totally unsuitable, but listed anyway. It is an enjoyable word-puzzle to solve!

'williamshakespeare' found words (alphabetical listing):

ah, am, amp, ampere, ape, are, as, ash, ashes, ask, asks, asp, ass, ear, epee, hap, hare, has, he, hear, her, here, he's, I, ill, I'll, is, lake, lakes, lamp, lap, lash, lashes, lass, Lear, leer, liar, lie, lies, like, likes, limp, lip, lisp, make, maker, makes, map, mare, mere, par, pare, pear, per, pre, sake, sakes, sap, sea, sere, shake, shakes, shape, shaper, share, she, sheer, she's spar, spare, spear, wake, wakes, war, ware, was, wash, washer, washes, wasp, were, where, wile, wiles, wilier, will, wish, wishes (87 words found)

Now use the same routine as outlined on p. 79, to foreground some letters and to push others into the background.

The results are immediately impressive. We've added a title, in the spirit of Edwin Morgan, to contrast with our text and our found poem.

Pygmalion

williamshakespeare

williamshakespeare

williamshakespeare

williamshakespeare

williamshakespeare

williamsha**ake**speare

williams**hak**espeare

willi**am**shakespeare

w**il**liamshakespeare

williamshakespeare

williamsh**ak**espeare

Translated from its real context it would read:

Pygmalion
I am a map,
A shaper, a maker
I make her as I wish her.

To get started, you may wish to present your class with a fully worked list. Use the one above, perhaps.

Once everyone has caught the idea, you could set homework, or a competition, to find as many words as possible in other numinous names, book titles, sayings, and quotations – thus forming new quarries to work on as creative sources for fresh Edwin Morgan-style found poems.

Your IWB

Foregrounding text using Word is very easy to do – but you need to have access to the keyboard. It's not really something that can be done easily straight on the IWB. If you hold down the Ctrl key, you can ask pupils to come to the front to do the double-click selection of words, but they need to be quite accurate. Be prepared for a little bit of fumbling.

Final words

Animating text using Word needs to be developed pedagogically. Work on why you're doing it, and exactly what effects you're after. The rewards are there to be harvested!

Chapter 16

Ordering our thoughts

Overview

It's not uncommon for a lively class discussion to grind to a halt once students learn that they have to produce a written response of some kind. While an IWB won't do the work for them, it can make organising and modelling a writing task much clearer. Fleeting thoughts can be captured on the board and then sifted and sorted to produce the outline of a text.

The board also offers a way to demonstrate means of planning an answer to increase the effectiveness of a student's argument.

Interactive whiteboard technology enables you and your students to do all of the following:

- prepare and present discussion topics and supporting information clearly;
- add comments, alternative views and further information as a result of discussion;
- sort arguments into categories and prioritise them;
- plan a written response by organising material visually and demonstrating how to revise ideas for better effect;
- save the results of class discussions for a subsequent lesson or for students to take away to use when writing their own responses.

These effects can be obtained, to a limited extent, by using a word processor or presentation software such as PowerPoint. However, neither of these is so easy to use and display in a classroom situation as an interactive whiteboard with its dedicated software.

LESSON IDEAS

1. For and against

The topic of this discussion is about parents taking children to school by car. You may want to choose your own discussion question to suit your class. There might,

`⟳ ✕ | ⬚⬚⬚⬚⬚ ⟱ | ⬚ | ▶ ✎ ✎⬚ ✎ ✐ ✗ ✦ △ ⬚ ✐ ‡`

Should parents be discouraged from driving their children to school?

pollution   'I'm not well!'

'I hate the school bus'   'I live too far away'

Mum drives past anyway   The roads are too dangerous

unhealthy   traffic jams

selfishness   accident risks

'I've got too much stuff to carry'

for example, be a topic in the news or a local issue that will engage your students more effectively. An open-ended question which will generate lively debate without having a clear-cut answer is best. Have a number of conflicting responses to a question in reserve, in case students close down the debate too early.

As the discussion develops, record additional arguments on the interactive whiteboard. You could also have further pages with appropriate illustrations or evidence such as newspaper headlines or quotations.

Once you have covered a range of ideas, ask the class to help sort them.

You may divide the board into simply 'for' and 'against' and ask students to decide where each point should go. They can come up to the board and drag the word or phrase to one side or the other. They will probably find that some comments don't fit easily into either category and that therefore there are some additional questions to be considered.

This could also be a good time to sift opinion from fact. For example, what is meant by the claim that some people are selfish over this issue? Are there examples of opinions expressed as fact?

Put the different points for different sides of the argument on separate pages to demonstrate skills in essay planning or expositional writing. This should simply be a matter of creating a new page for each view and then dragging the relevant words or phrases from the first page onto the next. Make sure each page has a suitable heading so students can see how the material is being organised into a coherent argument.

Should parents be discouraged from driving their children to school?

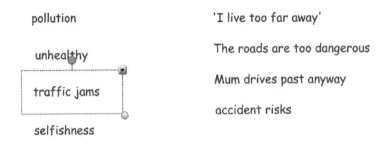

pollution

'I live too far away'

unhealthy

The roads are too dangerous

Mum drives past anyway

traffic jams

accident risks

selfishness

'I hate the school bus'

'I've got too much stuff to carry'

'I'm not well!'

Dividing the material up in this way makes it simple to show how to control the way an argument unfolds by swapping the order of the sections. This can be done by dragging the page thumbnails around in the page sorter view. Invite students to consider whether they want to make their own view clear from the beginning or save this to the end: the IWB should enable you quickly to show how this might look.

Tips

- Colour code points to help in sorting them.
- Give students opportunities to use the board as much as possible, including writing their own views. Use the handwriting recognition tool to convert comments into text for clarity and for later use.
- You could also demonstrate the use of suitable connectives.
- If students are going to take away a printed copy, print several interactive whiteboard 'pages' on one A4 sheet.
- Emphasise that students need to come to their own conclusions. Modelling should not give them the impression that there is only one answer to a question or a right way to write an answer.

2. Taking it further

If computers are available, students could follow this up by taking the material used to start the debate and organising it to present their own response to the topic. They could supplement the information already provided with their own ideas or research. You could, for example, provide more background information on additional pages or links to a few Internet sites, with clear guidance on how to use them. Students could be given copies of debating points or some starter questions. If appropriate, you might want to give further opportunities for feedback to the whole class to allow for further drafting and re-drafting.

If computers are not available, students could work on paper, with the material left visible on screen to guide them. If they are going to complete the task for homework or in a later lesson, you could print out the appropriate whiteboard page or pages as guidance.

This can be done as a whole-class discussion or with students working in groups before sharing ideas. You may want simply to present the question and record students' suggestions, or offer one or more prompts already on screen, for example:

Considerations

How would it be enforced?
Discouraged or forbidden?
What about special cases?
Would it affect who came to this school?

If you wish to model essay-writing in more detail, demonstrate how to write topic sentences for each paragraph. If the points you have collected merit more than one paragraph, simply drag some of them onto another page to create additional paragraphs. You could even have some ready-made topic sentences for students to choose from.

Chapter 17

Pictures to inspire

Words can inspire, but so can images – and in a visually busy world, pictures can often evoke responses in students which are different or more powerful than those inspired by words, memory or imagination alone.

The IWB offers opportunities both to manipulate images efficiently and to store outline ideas for later use.

LESSON IDEAS

1. Linking images

One way to stimulate creative narratives which will not be repetitions of other stories, forcing young writers to abandon plots or even themes which quite possibly they have seen elsewhere, is to set up a visual image bank using the IWB and create links from one image to another.

You can use images from any source, whether from the bank of pictures provided as part of your IWB resources, Windows clip art or the other hundred and one galleries available. For the purposes of this activity, though, it is wise to stick to fairly simple images and ones which are not large in terms of memory. You want to be able to load them quickly and move them around easily: small cartoon-style drawings are perfect.

Paste a selection onto your IWB and make them all of a similar size. A mixture of objects and people may be a good way to start, but if you wish to avoid prejudging the characters in your story, omit the people.

Ask students to look at the images and then think about how two or three of them might be connected in a story. Their narrative could be as simple as: 'A girl was walking down the street when she heard a bang. A man had fallen off his bicycle'. They should tell this short story to a partner, and the

partner asks three questions about the story which the student must answer. For example: Where is she going? Why did the man fall off the bike? Was he hurt? Previous practice in asking open rather than closed questions will be useful here.

Students then swap around and do the same thing. After this, you can:

- hear a selection of stories
- ask each pair to combine their stories
- ask students to add another image to their story.

You can go on adding images, of course, until you feel there is enough substance to a story to warrant its being written down. Alternatively, the stories can be told – and perhaps recorded – but need not be written at all in order to encourage and develop speaking and listening skills.

2. Collaborative writing

In this variation, ask students to think about how they might link the various items together, and then take feedback orally. Arrange the items as they appear in the story and begin to create the narrative. Leave gaps where you feel that the story needs fleshing out. Details of punctuation can be added later; what is important – and relies on a teacher's judgement and experience – is the points at which additional material would assist the story, its nature and extent. Some stories have too little detail; some have too much or irrelevant detail. Do we need to know how the cyclist was dressed? Probably not, though a detail such as 'there was a small bloodstain on the sleeve of his green

Amanda was on her way to visit her auntie who lived
across the town in ....

As she walked down the High Street she heard a loud
bang, like .... She turned around and saw.........

Oh dear he said, I have to deliver this clock part to my
friend this morning or ....

I could do that, she said. It's near where my auntie lives.

jersey where his arm had grazed the kerb' might add just enough to make the
tale seem believable.

To share the writing and the thinking as you go along is a powerful tool in
teaching and learning. As you model the process, drawing on students' ideas,
changing your mind, making small improvements, you are making explicit the
process of writing – something students experience too rarely.

Tips

- When selecting images for this activity, do not try to gather ones which
  seem to go together. Be as random as you can so that there is no obvious
  direction for the story or stories.
- Do not assume that this is merely a tool for younger or less able writers;
  it can be used with adults too.

3. Picture to poem

Images can be used in other ways to stimulate creative writing, of course. Good descriptive writing might be kindled by a single image such as a painting by J. M. W. Turner or Johannes Vermeer: very different subject matter, but equally powerful in their own ways. Paintings often work better than photographs for some reason, perhaps because they are less specific and allow the writer more imaginative space.

It can be difficult to explain to students what you want them to do. You certainly do not want to simply say 'Write a poem'. One way into this is to display a picture and, again, model some responses with a leaning towards imaginative description and use of figurative language.

These might be sentences or phrases, sometimes very short:

> The sea reflects the yellow sunlight like the yolk of a broken egg – ragged red clouds torn across the sky – lonely figures – the ungainly outline of the towers

Let students play around with these ways of expressing reactions to the image and then let them have a go at a fresh image without any teacher input.

From this reservoir of words, a powerful description or a short poem can often emerge. Students should feel free to make what they like of the words they have come up with and not to feel dissatisfied if nothing in a particular form seems to work. Sensitive guidance can be helpful, for you will be able to spot possibilities which they do not; nevertheless, it is the student's piece of work and their decisions have to be accepted.

Chapter 18

Transforming texts

To recognise differences between texts, students need to focus on specific language features. Transforming a text is an explicit way of demonstrating this. For example, turning direct speech into indirect speech makes the features of the text that have to change immediately apparent.

The biggest advantage of using ICT to transform texts is that the whole text does not have to be rewritten. We can focus solely on the crucial language features. Parts of the original can just be re-used. For example, when changing a text from present to past tense only the verbs will need altering.

Transformations might include past to present tense; narrative to diary entry; third person to first person; story to play; advice to persuasion; story to newspaper article; text book to advertisement; display advert to website page . . . the list is endless.

LESSON IDEAS

1. Private diary

Display the following diary entry, which is going to be changed into opening of a story written in the third person.

15th May

Dear diary

> It happened again: other children laughed when the register was called. I can't help it if my name is Janice Squid. I know it's a ridiculous name but there's nothing I can do about it.

> Sometimes it seems like you are my only friend so I will tell you about some other people who have stupid names: my family. Squids have always been private detectives. It runs in the blood. My grandfather solved the famous 'Seared Bodies' case.

Changes to the first paragraph might take this form:

> At the start of the following term it happened again: other children laughed when the register was called. She couldn't help it if her name was Janice Squid. She knew it was a ridiculous name but there was nothing she could do about it.

This is not as easy a task as might be assumed, and the process needs modelling carefully. The whiteboard is an excellent way to do this, as you can not only make the changes (using student input) but also keep a record to show where those alterations have occurred.

The activity can be carried out in reverse by changing a story into a diary entry:

> Janice moped around her office, hoping somebody would telephone her. She jumped at every noise she heard. Suddenly there was a knock at the door.
>
> When she opened the outer entry to the office, a tall woman dressed all in black confronted her.
>
> 'I am Mrs Black,' the stranger announced
>
> 'And I am Mrs White,' Janice thought, but she didn't say so. Instead, she indicated a chair and invited Mrs Black to sit down.
>
> 'I hope you will forgive my intrusion, but I think my life is in danger,' whispered Mrs Black.

The change to a diary entry will necessitate the use of reported speech, which often causes difficulty. Again, the IWB is a perfect way to demonstrate the kinds of changes needed; and if students have access to computers, a word processor offers them an ideal way to try it for themselves.

Tips

- Once transformations are complete, students might act out the rest of the conversation in pairs before continuing the diary.
- Investigate a section of a novel or short story to see which tenses are being used and why, particularly focusing on when a writer changes tenses. They can then make better choices about what tenses to use in their own writing.

2. The play's the thing

A good way to focus on character and direction in a play is to work on transforming a short section of dialogue into prose. Model the activity first. This is particularly important if you are working with an extract from a Shakespeare play, in order to emphasise that they are not required to render the speech into contemporary language but merely to insert the words that are additional to the dialogue in any story.

For example, here is an extract from *Romeo and Juliet*:

> ROMEO [Approaching Juliet.]
> If I profane with my unworthiest hand
> This holy shrine, the gentle sin is this:
> My lips, two blushing pilgrims, ready stand
> To smooth that rough touch with a tender kiss.
>
> JULIET Good pilgrim, you do wrong your hand too much,
> Which mannerly devotion shows in this;
> For saints have hands that pilgrims' hands do touch,
> And palm to palm is holy palmers' kiss.
>
> ROMEO Have not saints lips, and holy palmers too?
>
> JULIET Ay, pilgrim, lips that they must use in prayer.

Which can be quite easily transformed into prose, for example:

> Romeo sidled up to Juliet and took her hand. She was about to protest but softened when he spoke. 'If I profane with my unworthiest hand this holy shrine, the gentle sin is this: my lips, two blushing pilgrims, ready stand to smooth that rough touch with a tender kiss.'
>
> Juliet repressed a smile and tried to look stern. 'Good pilgrim,' she said, 'you do wrong your hand too much, which mannerly devotion shows in this; for saints have hands that pilgrims' hands do touch, and palm to palm is holy palmers' kiss.'
>
> Romeo held her hand more firmly and whispered, 'Have not saints lips, and holy palmers too?'
>
> 'Ay, pilgrim,' she replied, 'lips that they must use in prayer.'

Different interpretations of the text will arise from this lesson. If it is carried out as a class activity, these can be discussed as you go along. Does Romeo act confidently or is there a nervousness that could be expressed? In our version

Juliet is amused, but her responses could be made to sound more distant with very small changes to the text. If students work on a passage by themselves or in pairs, share some of the outcomes so that a similar discussion can be had.

As well as working at a textual level, students will be drawn in to a discussion of character and interpretation. Hopefully, they will begin to appreciate how much depends on the way that words are said, especially in the staging of a play – and particularly with Shakespeare.

Finally

Transforming texts is easy to prepare and deliver, yet powerful for helping learning because it focuses minds on the essential features of the text. Transformations work especially well as starters and do not have to take up the whole lesson.

Chapter 19

Counterpoint with PowerPoint

Using PowerPoint as a dramatic component in the performance of a text

PowerPoint was invented to support business presentations and sales pitches – the software shows its origins very clearly, with a preference for bullet points, tables and charts. However, we shouldn't allow the default designs of the program to divert us; it is good to be as creative as possible within the constraints imposed by legibility and manageability.

The concept of 'PowerPoint counterpoint' applies PowerPoint tangentially. PowerPoint normally acts as a giant communal place-marker on the screen – an aide-memoire for the speaker; and for the listeners, it is a method of emphasising and reinforcing the structural organisation of the talk. Why not use PowerPoint to run counter to the speaker(s)? It could make contradictory statements or emphasise points that are off-piste or inject images that disturb the predictable shape of the talk.

Used like this, PowerPoint becomes an autonomous component of the performance, not just its slavish supporter.

Lesson overview

The context is this: the class are working in groups on a performance of a key Shakespeare scene. The task is a dramatic reading of the text. Assuming access to computers, the class can program PowerPoint as a dramatic component of the work.

The PowerPoint slides can:

- flatly contradict the speakers' lines;
- introduce an image that runs counter to the intentions of the character speaking (for instance, Macbeth might be saying something sweet and friendly when a snake or a shark comes up on the screen, betraying his hidden thoughts);

- pick out key words or ideas and write them large across the screen;
- animate words and images appropriately to suit the action of the drama;
- inject quotations from another part of the play, or another work altogether (for instance, expand a reference to the Bible or classical literature);
- introduce the thoughts of the characters in thought-bubbles: if two characters are on stage at the same time, the thought bubble could show what the silent character is thinking while listening to the other (for instance, a conversation between Macbeth and Banquo).

Each group studies the passage, brainstorms the counter-pointing possibilities, writes the PowerPoint slides and then rehearses the timings of slide-changes, adjusting material until a satisfying performance is achieved. When they are ready, each group comes to the front of the class and performs the show. A useful conclusion would be to ask each group to stay in place after the drama and explain the rationale behind the effects – for example, why was an image of a shark introduced at that precise moment?

If the class has immediate access to computers, the work on preparing the PowerPoint slides can run in parallel to discussion and development.

If they do not have immediate access to computers, each group can write their ideas on photocopies of the target text, ready for transcription at a later time.

Tips

- Do not allow the PowerPoint part of the performance to upstage the oral delivery. Emphasise that the computer is not the main focus, and that the other aspects of the dramatic reading will be marked first (clarity, emphasis, emotion, timing, etc.).
- Explore the animations available in PowerPoint. For instance, it is perfectly possible to make an image of a spider crawl from one side of the screen to the other, and then a little later to make the word 'spider' do exactly the same, followed a little later by the word 'Iago' – visually tying ideas together through a sort of visual rhyme scheme.
- Discourage sound effects and extreme animations unless there is a compelling argument for them. 'Keep it subtle' is the best rule.

Preparation and resources

The text of Shakespeare's plays and most classical literature is readily available on the Internet – you won't have to type anything in. Microsoft clip art has plenty of excellent materials to exploit – see if you can have it installed and always available on the classroom machines. Google will also furnish you with thousands of images – but some school networks restrict this resource. Copy a stock of suitable images at home, if this is the case.

Your IWB

The interactive whiteboard software will achieve some of the effects in PowerPoint, and it may be worth playing with it to assess its potential. In particular, if you choose to use Internet-derived images as opposed to clip art, you'll discover that Notebook and Flipchart will manipulate graphics very cleverly, whereas PowerPoint will not allow you to set transparencies and other essential effects.

Final words

PowerPoint used in this ironic way will re-energise the class's interest in a possibly overused program that they nevertheless all feel able to drive. The talk associated with the texts-behind-the-text is educational gold – get ready to record oral work and be prepared for some startlingly good insights.

Chapter 20

Show, look and disappear

PowerPoint, combined with your IWB, can become a powerful tool to engage attention and encourage questioning. Curiosity is a strong motivator. Texts which might be viewed with disdain or lack of interest become more engaging when hidden, coded or otherwise made difficult to access – or hold on to. Mystery texts and hidden texts exploit this characteristic.

PowerPoint offers some interesting variations on this theme, given its variety of entrance and exit effects. If a text is only visible for a short time, students must pay attention. Once the text has disappeared, discussion can follow, picking up on which elements have been remembered.

The basic technique is explained here with a simple example. The writing to be examined is a non-fiction text from a pack enclosing a powdered chocolate drink.

Indulge your love of chocolate with Silky-Choc – the ultimate hot chocolate, made from luscious flakes of milk chocolate.

For a deliciously creamy drink add 6-heaped teaspoonsful of Silky-Choc flakes to a large cup of hot milk. Stir the flakes until dissolved. Sprinkle a few more flakes on top of the drink before serving. For an even creamier drink, top your cup of Silky-Choc with whipped cream and sprinkle more flakes.

We want you to enjoy this product. Should you have any queries or suggestions regarding Silky-Choc or not be entirely satisfied, please return this product with the packaging to the address below, stating where and when it was purchased.

Paste the text, a paragraph at a time, into a PowerPoint slide.

Different types of texts

- Indulge your love of chocolate with Silky-Choc – the ultimate hot chocolate, made from luscious flakes of milk chocolate.
- For a deliciously creamy drink add 6-heaped teaspoonsful of Silky-Choc flakes to a large cup of hot milk. Stir the flakes until dissolved. Sprinkle a few more flakes on top of the drink before serving.
- For an even creamier drink, top your cup of Silky-Choc with whipped cream and sprinkle more flakes.

Select Animations and choose 'Appear'.

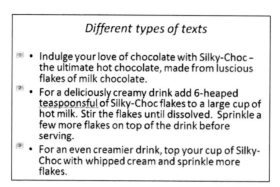

Now go to the Animation Pane on the right of the screen and click the down arrow. Select 'Effect Options'.

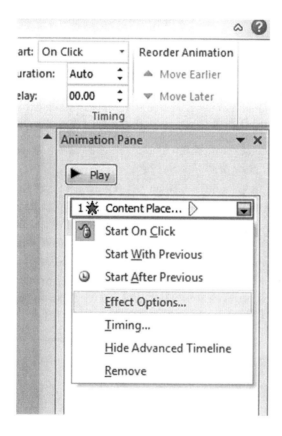

In the dialogue box, select 'Hide After Animation' and 'By word'.

When you show the slide, each paragraph should appear word by word and then disappear. For example, here we see the second paragraph half way through its revelation.

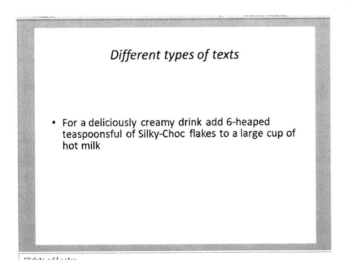

LESSON IDEAS

I. Simple recall

Students are asked to jot down words they remember. Use a variation of the 'Boggle' scoring method, whereby any correctly recalled word receives one point; any correct word which only three people have got scores 2; only two people scores 3; and a uniquely recalled word scores 4. Individual wipe-clean boards are ideal for this.

Discuss which words were most easily recalled and those which were not recalled at all. Did they remember practical words such as cup and milk, or descriptive/persuasive ones such as luscious? This is an opportunity to give some attention to vocabulary and to spelling in a context which makes them a little more interesting.

2. Which type of text?

Display a selection of words from a text to be examined. Using the chocolate drink extract, you might choose to show these:

> below cup deliciously dissolved flakes indulge love luxury purchased quality satisfied sprinkle suggestions top ultimate want whipped

Use the same game approach and ask what kind of text they think these words might be derived from – and why. You can point out that this particular text combines elements of at least three different text types: instruction, information and persuasion! Display the original text and discuss how the manufacturer has used language to promote the product.

It would be useful to have a number of similar texts available so that comparisons can be made.

3. Poems and story extracts

You can use the 'Show, look and disappear' technique to display a poem to be studied or revised. Similarly, an extract from a story or a play could be shown, followed by some recall questions. Students could be allowed to make notes as the text is displayed: a useful way to train them to look out for key facts and phrases.

Tips

- Use software tools available with your IWB to annotate texts, marking key words, and linking related words or those which have been misunderstood.
- Use the technique to display your lesson objectives or a particularly important point you wish students to remember. This will probably get more attention than if you just wrote or spoke to the class.

Chapter 21

Movie capture animation

Using the movie capture software that comes with a whiteboard to create simple animations

Interactive whiteboard software frequently comes with the facility to 'record'. In effect a video is created, enabling you to replay everything you've done on the screen, including commentary if you have a microphone plugged in. You can see every movement of the cursor, all changes of screen and movement or adjustment of graphics, faithfully repeated. This feature can be exploited creatively.

Lesson overview

First find and experiment with the video capture capabilities of your version of whiteboard. Don't despair: if there isn't video capture on your whiteboard, you can find free software, or buy highly effective programs that will do the job – for instance, Camtasia from Techsmith.com (free trials, but expensive to buy).

It's usually easy to get started. You have a tape recorder-type interface, with the usual red button for record and the rightward pointing triangle to indicate play. You simply click on the red button and then proceed with your screen activities as normal. If you want to explain a complicated procedure, you can talk into a microphone and the program will impose the soundtrack on the screen movements. When you play it back, it's like having someone sitting by you to show you how to do something on the computer.

Try the following:

- Put up a poem on the screen.
- Set the recorder going.
- Talk through the poem, using the arrow pointer to indicate words, underlining some words, highlighting others.
- Stop the recorder.
- Press play.

You'll see your whole 'lesson' replayed.

How might you apply this simple first step in class? Well, we wouldn't recommend pre-programmed lessons – it's a thousand times more effective to do it live! But what about packaging the resultant movies as revision material for iPods and portable devices? Try it (the screen capture software often has a facility for saving in mobile-friendly formats): does it still work on the small screens? Or even better, let students work in groups and then ask them to record their discussions for replay to the whole class.

Now try extending the idea.

Set the recorder going when groups of students are working on pieces of writing, using individual computers. Every hesitation, alteration, deletion and addition will be recorded alongside the discussion that accompanies the editing. When the movies are replayed for the class at the end of the lesson, each group can reflect on their writing and the decisions that went into it. They can add to the commentary by attempting to explain the thinking more fully. An ideal task for this stage would be the reduction of a highly descriptive piece of prose to a very compressed format (like a haiku, or a word-limited piece of 50 words).

Finally, you might want to try a form of crude animation.

- Place a graphic object on the screen.
- Set the recorder going.
- Drag the graphic from one place to another, or re-size the picture – while reading lines of Shakespeare – and with a bit of fiddling you can use the image as a marionette.
- Stop the recorder and replay – you'll see all the movements faithfully repeated.

Once you have established the basic techniques, groups can attempt to script and story-board such animations, working on backgrounds or effects like having a character approach by simply re-sizing from small to large.

This is crude, rough stuff – but it's the quick-and-dirty instantly do-able end of the game. If you want to take things further, and you have the money to buy into dedicated software (usually expensive), you can progress upward and onward. But most of the basic ideas can be replicated in this use of Movie Capture. It's also a lot quicker than stop-motion animation, which will devour countless (albeit very satisfying) hours.

Your IWB

Smartboards and Promethean boards have built-in video capture utilities which record the whole screen and everything that happens on it. They are ideal for this purpose.

Final words

The activity follows this pattern: work on a task; personally reflect on the process; analyse the learning collectively. As such, it matches the very latest techniques in encouraging self-reflective and aware learners. Try to build up practice around these ideas – they will pay you very rich dividends!

Index